FILLING THE EMPTY PLACES

Beneth Peters Jones

JOURNEYFORTH

Greenville, South Carolina

Library of Congress Cataloging-in-Publication Data

Jones, Beneth Peters,
    Filling the empty places / Beneth Peters Jones.
        p. cm.
    Summary: "Filling the Empty Places challenges women to explore their
problems honestly and move toward a scriptural solution"—Provided by
publisher.
    ISBN-13: 978-1-59166-781-0 (perfect bound pbk. : alk. paper)
    1. Christian women—Religious life. I. Title.
    BV4527.J663 2007
    248.8'43—dc22

                                                              2007037844

Cover Photo Credit: Craig Oesterling

Robert Frost: "The Road Not Taken" from THE POETRY OF ROBERT
FROST edited by Edward Connery Lathem. Copyright 1916, 1969 by Henry
Holt and Company, copyright 1944 by Robert Frost. Reprinted by permission of
Henry Holt and Company, LLC.

Author unknown: "Lean Hard." Taken from Streams in the Desert® by Mrs.
Charles Cowman; James G. Reimann. Copyright © 1997 by Zondervan. Used by
permission of Zondervan.

The fact that materials produced by other publishers may be referred to in this
volume does not constitute an endorsement of the content or theological position
of materials produced by such publishers.

All Scripture is quoted from the Authorized King James Version.

Filling the Empty Places

Cover design by Rita Golden
Page design and layout by Kelley Moore

© 2007 by BJU Press
Greenville, South Carolina 29614
JourneyForth Books is a division of BJU Press

Printed in the United States of America

ISBN 978-1-59166-781-0

15 14 13 12 11 10 9 8 7 6 5 4 3 2 1

My heart honors the special friends
God has graciously given through the years—
those women of the Lord with whom
I've been able to spend too little time.

But they have illustrated Christ's fullness
and have richly contributed to mine.
May each dear one know that
her name should be here.

CONTENTS

PREFACE

BETTER IS THE SIGHT OF THE EYES THAN THE WANDERING OF
THE DESIRE: THIS IS ALSO VANITY AND VEXATION OF SPIRIT.

ECCLESIASTES 6:9

She appeared to be in her late twenties; she assured me she knew
Christ as her Savior. She was married to a man who earned a
good living and was a loving husband. Her several small children
were all healthy. Yet tears welled in her eyes. While she briefly
acknowledged and expressed gratitude for her blessings, the bulk
of her conversation focused on her yearnings: freedom from the
house and the opportunity to be active in music. Her inmost self
so ached for fulfillment beyond her reach that she was on multiple tranquilizers prescribed by her physician. In our limited time
together, I shared Scripture principles and personal, concerned
encouragement. Then that dear young woman—with unsteady
steps—walked out of my life.

There had been a strong echo in my heart as I'd listened; the tale
of longing, confusion, guilt, frustration, and hurt replayed personal

memories as well as similar confessions by counselees. Within days, that particular young woman's outpouring served to finalize a year-long accumulation of thought, motivating me to begin writing *Filling the Empty Places*.

A woman who has come to normal adulthood knows the reality of empty places in life and in self. Wherever they are, vacuums of "wandering desire" raise questions; they demand response. The young woman who talked with me at that particular retreat had chosen the wrong response to her emptiness. Prescribed tranquilizers had glazed her eyes, slowed her reflexes, slurred her speech, and so compromised her physical balance that someone needed to stay near to steady her. They had done nothing at all to supply the peace and wholeness she sought.

We Christians claim that the Bible contains all the answers God intends for us to have in our earthly life. It does, indeed. However, we tend to appropriate Scripture with either a compartmentalized or "split-level" mentality. Compartmentalization makes the Bible a Sunday and (maybe) midweek text, assigning it to the "Reserve" shelf in our mental library. Split-level usage accesses the Word's instruction for broad, general "upper level" areas of life while ignoring its resources for our ground floor and basement levels—daily personal quandaries, intimate internal challenges, inmost longings, and unexpressed struggles.

By such hit-and-miss attention to God's Word we leave vast areas of self and life vulnerable to spiritual defeat.

Jesus Christ, the Living Word, said in John 10:10, "I am come that ye might have life, and that ye might have it more abundantly."

Abundant life is life that's richly blessed. But how many of us would honestly describe our daily experiences in such terms? Listen to your self-talk; hear what other women say and demonstrate: our empty places plague us.

I didn't have the opportunity for an extended time with that dear young woman at the retreat. How I wish it could have been otherwise! How I'd have treasured the opportunity, figuratively, to take her hand and walk with her, moving away from frustration toward fulfillment; from perplexity to peace; from yearning to yielding; from regret to rejoicing. The walk together would not—could not—have been via mortal brain power or experiential expertise. It would instead have been a mutual seeking of immortal wisdom and faith's vision.

Perhaps, however, that walk together can be realized to a certain degree because her heart cry has resulted in this writing. Too, perhaps by walking beside others—you—my desire to share God's help may be realized.

My hope is that there will be a twofold effect upon you, the reader: first, comfort from knowing you're not alone in difficulties engendered by your perceived needs, and, second, challenge to explore the problems honestly and move toward their scriptural solution. Moreover, I would plead with you to allow all corners of your mind and heart to become transparent as you read and respond.

As I've prayed throughout the writing, so too I'll be praying as you read, that Jesus Christ may be revealed in His unlimited ability to fill not just one or some, but rather all of our *Empty Places*.

> For he satisfieth the longing soul, and filleth the hungry soul with goodness. (Psalm 107:9)

THE ESSENTIAL EMPTINESS

THEN SHALL THE DUST RETURN TO THE EARTH AS IT WAS:
AND THE SPIRIT SHALL RETURN UNTO GOD WHO GAVE IT.
VANITY OF VANITIES, SAITH THE PREACHER, ALL IS VANITY.

ECCLESIASTES 12:7–8

King Solomon, who wrote those words, was the wisest man who ever lived. God imparted unequaled wisdom in answer to Solomon's prayer. Second Chronicles 1:11–12 records the special moment:

> And God said to Solomon, Because this was in thine heart, and thou hast not asked riches, wealth, or honour, nor the life of thine enemies, neither yet hast asked long life, but hast asked wisdom and knowledge for thyself, that thou mayest judge my people, over whom I have made thee king: wisdom and knowledge is granted unto thee; and I will give thee riches, wealth, and honour such as none of the kings have had that have been before thee, neither shall there any after thee have the like.

As he moved on from that moment of God's gifting, Solomon probed for life's meaning. As he explored various aspects of human existence, he repeatedly noted "vanity," or emptiness. Just as Solomon addressed the transience of our earthly walk, so the Bible as a whole often speaks of life's brevity.

Typically, the fleeting nature of our days doesn't become personally evident and meaningful until we transition from our teens to our twenties. Then the seemingly endless, can't-wait-to-grow-up period suddenly abandons us to maturity, with its responsibilities and its rush.

In childhood we are literalists, conscious of and comfortable with that which can be seen, touched, heard, or tasted. But even in maturity as you and I travel rapidly along our short earthly pathways, we still seem better able to handle life's tangibles than its intangibles.

Visible entities, of course, do not make up all of life's reality. We recognize earth, plants, and animals as being real, and we respond to them as may be necessary and prudent. Yet another natural—but invisible—entity, wind, also acts upon and affects us. Our responses to it may be quite different because of its mysterious, invisible nature.

Scripture addresses the mystery of wind in John 3:8—

> The wind bloweth where it listeth, and thou hearest the sound thereof, but canst not tell whence it cometh, and whither it goeth.

Jesus Christ spoke those words; in them we are reminded that there are different types of reality. No one has ever or will ever see wind. We know its presence, direction, and intensity only through its effects upon visible things—trees, clouds, bushes, and so forth. Nevertheless, not one of us would deny wind's existence.

This book will address one of the invisible realities we commonly experience: unmet needs. We'll focus specifically on the empty places that seem most to challenge Christian women, needs that are not primarily physical or material, though in some instances there may be observable connections.

How do we become aware of nonphysical, nonmaterial needs? We sense them. Let's liken those sensory impressions to winds— winds carrying a message of emptiness.

These breezes may blow in childhood. A child in an openly un- happy home, for example, experiences constant, moaning winds of emotional need. Conversely, a youngster who is surfeited with toys, endlessly and expensively entertained, and only loosely disciplined may know whispering winds of ache for genuine parental love.

Although no chilling winds may blow in childhood days, we become wind-aware as adults when maturity teaches us of life's imperfections. We experience the winds issuing from our empty places in varying degrees of clarity and strength. They may be oc- casional breezes—brief, vague stirrings of longing that whisper empty . . . empty . . . empty. In other instances they are high-velocity winds—recurrent shouts of empty . . . empty . . . empty! They may be tornado-force gales—shaking, aching desires that wrack our in- nermost being.

A Different Focus

The unsaved world strongly focuses upon humanity's empty places. From that focus come psychology, psychiatry, and psychotherapy with endless theories, varied extremes of treatment, and outland- ish inferences and conclusions. Perhaps because of the resultant psychobabble, born-again Christians tend to trivialize the problem of unmet needs. Yet who should better be able to identify, analyze, and prescribe for this human malady? Whereas secular practition- ers are limited to human theories and treatments, Christians have the Bible—the ultimate reference work, whose eternal Author not only states His creation of our humanity but also gives His accurate diagnoses and effective prescriptions for our maladies.

THE CENTRAL EMPTINESS

The eternally important empty place is the God-shaped void that exists within every human soul. As long as the soul's core need remains unmet, any others can know only superficial supply. God's design is that our aching spiritual empty place should draw us to salvation in His dear Son, Jesus Christ. When we rightly make that choice, we come into possession of life's greatest treasure.

> How excellent is thy lovingkindness, O God! therefore the children of men put their trust under the shadow of thy wings. They shall be abundantly satisfied with the fatness of thy house; and thou shalt make them drink of the river of thy pleasures. For with thee is the fountain of life: in thy light shall we see light. (Psalm 36:7–9)

I was nine years old when I personally accepted Jesus Christ as my Savior. I was the child of Christian parents. Our family faithfully attended a Bible-preaching church. However, I became aware that a great difference existed between me and the other members of my family. An indefinable but insistent breeze of longing originated in that internal empty place, and I listened with new intensity to Sunday school lessons and to the preacher's sermons.

The Holy Spirit turned on the light of Scripture and identified my emptiness—a God-vacant soul, marred by sin. Although nine may seem young, I intellectually understood my sinfulness. Nor will I ever forget the greatest, most convicting demonstration of my ugly sin nature.

Each of our various homes in Washington State was near a small town, and my father made sure every home site had enough acreage for him to indulge his hobby of raising chickens. That meant I was well acquainted with chickens at all stages from fertilized eggs to full-grown show cocks and hens. My favorites, of course, were the baby chicks. Adorable yellow puffballs with tiny, peeping voices, they provided me with many hours of entertainment. They also provided the opportunity for cruelty.

When we needed chicken for a meal, Daddy would select whatever most succulent-looking bird suited, hold it by its feet, and kill it with swift efficiency by dashing its head against some solid object.

One day I was in a black mood for some now-forgotten reason. Knowing that to express my feelings to anyone in the family would mean strong remonstrance or punishment, I stormed out to the baby chicks' pen. Kneeling beside it, my shadowed thoughts gathered, darkened, and ultimately focused upon those hapless chicks. I reached out, took one, held it by its feet, and swung its head against a nearby post. To this day memory re-creates the awful feeling of guilt and shame that swept over me in a nauseating flood. I burst into tears at the chick's death throes, then sat cradling its cooling body in my cupped hands, wishing vainly for its life to return.

My personal sinfulness was suddenly, sickeningly, and unmistakably evident. My heart's dark and empty hole was an awful chasm separating me from God's holiness. Let me share with you the sweet progression over the bridge of God's grace from sin's emptiness to salvation's filling. That bridge has firm Scripture planks.

My sinful heart was not just hateful in my sight; it was an abomination to God. In His holiness He couldn't look at me with acceptance, but only with condemnation.

> Your iniquities have separated between you and your God, and your sins have hid his face from you, that he will not hear. (Isaiah 59:2)

> For all have sinned, and come short of the glory of God. (Romans 3:23)

> He that believeth not is condemned already, because he hath not believed in the name of the only begotten Son of God. (John 3:18)

My sinfulness was both a human condition and a personal responsibility.

> He that believeth on the Son hath everlasting life: and he that believeth not the Son shall not see life: but the wrath of God abideth on him. (John 3:36)

> For as in Adam all die, even so in Christ shall all be made alive. (I Corinthians 15:22)

> Know ye not that the unrighteous shall not inherit the kingdom of God? Be not deceived: neither fornicators, nor idolators, nor adulterers, nor effeminate, nor abusers of themselves with mankind, nor thieves, nor covetous, nor drunkards, nor revilers, nor extortioners, shall inherit the kingdom of God. (I Corinthians 6:9–10)

God's justice demanded judgment and punishment.

> The soul that sinneth, it shall die. (Ezekiel 18:4)

Despite my sinful ugliness, the great God of love spoke wooingly to my heart.

> Come now, and let us reason together, saith the Lord: though your sins be as scarlet, they shall be as white as snow; though they be red like crimson, they shall be as wool. (Isaiah 1:18)

There was no way I could span the gulf between me and God.

> For whosoever shall keep the whole law, and yet offend in one point, he is guilty of all. (James 2:10)

> Not by works of righteousness which we have done, but according to His mercy He saved us. (Titus 3:5)

> Knowing that a man is not justified by the works of the law, but by the faith of Jesus Christ, even we have believed in Jesus Christ, that we might be justified by the faith of Christ, and not

by the works of the law: for by the works of the law shall no flesh be justified. (Galatians 2:16)

I had to lay aside whatever human thinking or striving might allure me and cast myself entirely upon God's mercy.

For there is one God, and one mediator between God and men, the man Christ Jesus. (I Timothy 2:5)

For he hath made him to be sin for us, who knew no sin, that we might be made the righteousness of God in him. (II Corinthians 5:21)

I had to reach with empty hands to accept God's gift of salvation. In that instant an eternal transaction was wrought by His grace.

The blood of Jesus Christ his Son, cleanseth us from all sin. (I John 1:7)

And you, being dead in your sins and the uncircumcision of your flesh, hath he quickened together with him, having forgiven you all trespasses; blotting out the hand-writing of ordinances that was against us, which was contrary to us, and took it out of the way, nailing it to his cross. (Colossians 2:13–14)

But now in Christ Jesus ye who sometimes were far off are made nigh by the blood of Christ. (Ephesians 2:13)

And you, that were sometime alienated and enemies in your mind by wicked works, yet now hath he reconciled in the body of his flesh through death, to present you holy and unblameable and unreproveable in his sight. (Colossians 1:21–22)

A key factor in filling spiritual emptiness is responsive choice. That choice confronts every individual to whom Christ's gospel is presented. The Bible gives us portraits of those who made a wrong choice just as it shows those who chose rightly. The story of the rich young ruler (Matthew 19:16–22; Mark 10:17–22) is especially powerful because it focuses upon the emptiness that made him approach Jesus in the first place. Think through this familiar incident with me.

> There came one running, and kneeled to him, and asked him, Good Master, what shall I do that I may inherit eternal life? (Mark 10:17)

The passage later tells us "he had great possessions." Although his wealth is not described in detail, the term "great possessions" indicates that this fellow, though youthful, enjoyed a life that was full in terms of money, social standing, creature comforts, and personal possessions. He didn't casually amble up to Jesus and pose his question; he ran to the Lord and fell on his knees before Him. Only a great awareness of need would motivate such an approach in public. His full hands were as nothing compared to his empty heart.

In Mark 10:18, Jesus noted and challenged the questioner's form of address, immediately directing his focus to Himself as God. Then, in verse 19, Jesus listed the portion of the Ten Commandments that prescribe man-ward living. The young man replied with an amazing statement of his lifelong moral striving: "All these have I observed from my youth." His exemplary law keeping was apparently true since Jesus did not contradict the claim.

Matthew's record of the incident includes a detail that Mark omits. The man uttered a second question that though brief revealed the aching void he sensed deep within: "What lack I yet?"

His consistent striving since childhood for goodness in man-ward attitudes and acts had failed to give him peace. He could not escape a consciousness of having missed something essential. Jesus responded that the young man's one lack was Christ Himself.

Sadly, the young man went away from his encounter with Jesus as pitifully empty as when he arrived. He could have known fullness in heart, soul, and life from that moment forward, but he chose instead the material abundance that left his soul empty. There was no lack or failing in the Savior: the young man's emptiness—for time and for eternity—remained through his choice.

At another point in His earthly ministry Jesus presented a question to His hearers that highlights the tragic decision made by the rich young ruler and every other individual throughout history at his or her point of choice.

> For what shall it profit a man, if he shall gain the whole world, and lose his own soul? Or what shall a man give in exchange for his soul? (Mark 8:36–37)

The pages to follow can hold neither meaning nor help for the woman who has not accepted Jesus Christ as her personal Savior. I pray, therefore, that each reader in individual, private, and personal honesty, will obey the Scripture injunction:

> Examine yourselves, whether ye be in the faith; prove your own selves. Know ye not your own selves, how that Jesus Christ is in you, except ye be reprobate? (II Corinthians 13:5).

Deep personal probing must go beyond surface appearances, feelings, and habits:

- Your name on the church cradle roll
- Your front-row seat at church
- Your participation in the choir or the youth group or the women's missionary group
- Your generosity toward needy people and ministries
- Your careful, detailed attention to denominational standards and practices
- Your personal, strict preferences about dress, makeup, and hair

The only bridge over the flaming chasm of God's justice is the cross of Christ Jesus, the Lamb slain in substitution for you and me. Only Christ can erase our sin penalty and make us acceptable to

God. As we cross that bridge, we are marked with a double-sided seal of identity.

> Nevertheless the foundation of God standeth sure, having this seal. The Lord knoweth them that are his. And, let everyone that nameth the name of Christ depart from iniquity. (II Timothy 2:19)

Blessed indeed is the soul redeemed by the precious shed blood of Jesus Christ. That soul henceforth has an abiding assurance of eternal relationship, supply, and safety.

> For ye have not received the spirit of bondage again to fear; but ye have received the Spirit of adoption, whereby we cry, Abba, Father. The Spirit itself beareth witness with our spirit, that we are the children of God: and if children then heirs, heirs of God, and joint-heirs with Christ. (Romans 8:15–17)

Salvation makes heaven our glorious destiny. Earth, however, is our spiritual schoolroom. The lessons God would teach us are varied and challenging. The born-again believer, having had her sins forgiven, is a new creature. The freshness of spiritual life is a wonderful reality. It soon becomes evident, however, that though her soul is heaven bound, her mortal self is still earth anchored. Therein lies conflict—spiritual warfare. Recurring battles take place in the area of our perceived needs, or empty places.

ADDRESSING REALITIES

The purpose on every page hereafter is to present the only reliable, effective textbook for our learning as we deal with our empty places—the Bible.

> For whatsoever things were written aforetime were written for our learning, that we through patience and comfort of the scriptures might have hope. (Romans 15:4)

Great peace have they which love thy law; and nothing shall
offend them [cause them to stumble]. (Psalm 119:165)

The law of the Lord is perfect, converting the soul: the testimony
of the Lord is sure, making wise the simple. The statutes of
the Lord are right, rejoicing the heart: the commandment of
the Lord is pure, enlightening the eyes. The fear of the Lord
is clean, enduring for ever: the judgments of the Lord are true
and righteous altogether. More to be desired are they than gold,
yea, than much fine gold: sweeter also than honey and the
honeycomb. Moreover by them is thy servant warned: and in
keeping of them there is great reward. (Psalm 19:7–11)

The Bible is no ordinary book. It is God-breathed.

For the prophecy came not in old time by the will of man: but
holy men of God spake as they were moved by the Holy Ghost.
(II Peter 1:21)

The Bible is more than paper and ink and printed symbols. It is
a living book.

For the word of God is quick [alive], and powerful, and sharper
than any twoedged sword, piercing even to the dividing asunder
of soul and spirit, and of the joints and marrow, and is a discerner
of the thoughts and intents of the heart. (Hebrews 4:12)

The Bible is not a book whose message will fall into dust and
decay over time. Jesus Christ said of it:

Heaven and earth shall pass away, but my words shall not pass
away (Matthew 24:35).

The Bible is unique. It is alive not only in its ability to search out
and illuminate every part of our being but also in some way that lies
beyond our understanding, unified with Christ Himself.

And the Word was made flesh, and dwelt among us, (and we beheld his glory, the glory as of the only begotten of the Father,) full of grace and truth. (John 1:14)

So, then, when we turn to the Bible, we are in a real sense accessing the mind, the heart, and the hand of the Lord Jesus Christ. What would He have us learn about—and because of— our empty places?

CHAPTER TWO

THE NATURE OF EMPTINESS

HE THAT OBSERVETH THE WIND SHALL NOT SOW; AND HE THAT REGARDETH THE CLOUDS SHALL NOT REAP.

ECCLESIASTES 11:4

Ecclesiastes 11:4 can be applied positively and negatively. A farmer who briefly refrains from his sowing or reaping because of the weather may be doing the wise thing—insuring effective planting and nonwasteful harvesting. On the other hand, the farmer who stalls lengthily or permanently would be a miserable failure.

If we apply the analogy of wind as a messenger of needs, a Christian woman, like the farmer, is wise to recognize the wind but unwise to let it determine her life. Yet, sadly, many women are negatively marked, growth stunted, or severely limited due to winds of want.

"Want winds" blow from various parts of our being and our life. We announce our needs shortly after we're born. At first they are the basics—food and physical comfort. As we mature, however, our perceived needs multiply, expand, and become more sophisticated.

Thereafter, rather than audibly squalling to get someone's response to our simple physical necessity, we may weep voicelessly over an emptiness we can't even describe. Let's begin to consider how we may recognize winds that signal emptiness without letting them become deafening and defeating in our spiritual life.

Psalm 135:7 often finds its way into my consciousness: "He bringeth the wind out of his treasuries." God first used that phrase to rebuke my negative feelings about the windy weather in Greenville. For years I allowed the winds—which often mean horizontal delivery of drenching rains—to sour my attitude, curdle my relationships, and curtail outdoor activities. God's treasuries as the winds' source was a jolting concept; then it became an impetus for change. By extension, the truth of the Scripture phrase also speaks to the subject at hand.

We prefer that all our person and the whole of our pathway be filled with warmth, brightness, and calm. Wind is disquieting. Yet the psalmist wrote, "He bringeth the wind out of his treasuries." Just as God ordains wind meteorologically for His purposes, He also does so spiritually. Simple considerations of ordinary wind, and the lessons of acceptance, adjustment, and appreciation we learn from them are spiritually applicable.

Treasuries, of course, are storage places for great riches. Few people in any era of history or area of the world possess the kind of wealth that requires a treasury. Our knowledge of such abundance is limited to tales of past dynasties or of modern financial institutions. Immense material wealth challenges our ability to comprehend, yet all earthly accumulations of wealth become as nothing when we consider God's treasuries. Human mentality must simply stand in open-mouthed wonder, overwhelmed by the limitless resources the term indicates. God declares something of His limitless riches when He says,

For every beast of the forest is mine, and the cattle upon a thousand hills. I know all the fowls of the mountains: and the wild beasts of the field are mine. If I were hungry, I would not tell thee; for the world is mine, and the fullness thereof. (Psalm 50:10–12)

Wind's origination in God's treasuries should motivate us, then, to rejoice and be grateful. So why do I react with resentment, downheartedness, or complaint? Because my flesh automatically focuses upon itself: I dislike wind's disruptive effects on hair, clothing, items held in my hand. My last consideration is toward the Creator of the wind. What a shame that my *me* focus repeatedly blinds me to the *He* origination! The same holds true in things of the spirit. As Christian women, you and I fall into patterns of being and living. We get comfortable. It's as if our heart's hairdo is set to our liking . . . our soul's dress fits fairly well and impresses others . . . our hands' spiritual tasks are familiar and manageable. Then all at once along comes wind. It ruffles our hair, whips at our clothing, and threatens what we hold in our hands. At the same time, it sends a chill into our soul. Comfort gives place to unease.

Ah, yes, comfort. The human condition seeks comfort both internally and externally. Think for a moment about some of the ways we demonstrate that tendency.

As infants we react against discomfort, whether it be a chafed bottom or an empty tummy.

As children we cringe under the taunts of playmates or the teasing of adults.

As teens we seek the comfort of acceptance by our peers— sometimes in extremes of conformity.

As adults our yen for that which is comfortable operates in every area of our life—from the clothes we wear to the place we sit in church.

We opt for familiarity in our physical setting—we're shaken when things are out of place. We operate best in a familiar routine—we can be thrown off stride, for instance, by a malfunctioning alarm clock. We feel uncomfortable when thrust into a new social setting or a different culture. We tend toward the familiar in our work, feeling threatened by complications or challenges. We're uneasy when confronted by a viewpoint that opposes our own mindset.

A similar instinct for comfort operates in spiritual experience. The power of preference is seen in the great numbers of Christians accurately described by the phrase "saved, satisfied, and sitting." That's not what God desires. Instead, He wants each of us to be spiritually alive, growing toward personal Christlikeness, and presenting an effective testimony of life and lips to those around us. So He must disturb us somehow, get us off dead center. He often does that by sending disturbing winds—blustery messages of unmet needs.

The Origin of Emptiness

Although emptiness is a universal human experience, our great Creator God did not intend it to be so. His two original human beings—Adam and Eve—knew both internal and external fullness. God met their every need and walked with them in daily fellowship. Their relationship with each other and their circumstances reflected the fullness of their relationship with God. But Eden's perfection came under attack by the destroyer, Satan. He lied, maligned the character of God, and lured the creature to choose against the Creator.

God's gracious, loving heart equipped His human creatures with a free will. He did not want worship, fellowship, love, and obedience from robot beings but from those who could choose positive heart responses. Emptiness became a human reality through humanity's own wrong choices.

We're not told how long the man and woman enjoyed Eden's bliss. Eventually, however, Eve apparently walked off into the verdure alone. Have you ever really let your imagination re-create the moments that followed?

> The sun is shining, and its light through the orchard canopy dapples the earth's velvety green. As she looks about her, Eve sees every imaginable kind of fruit tree. The brightness of the fruits' colors pleases her eyes; the mingled aromas beautifully scent the air. What joy there is for her in the daily experience of that indescribably rich world. Her eyes sweep across the lovely panorama. She notices movement. What could that be? She stands on tiptoe, then bends first left and then right, trying to get a clearer view through the luxuriant undergrowth. Her heart begins to beat faster because she realizes that the intriguing movement is near the forbidden tree. She catches her breath, remembering Adam's warnings and her careful self-protective conduct in all the days past. And yet . . . Then it comes again—a rosy, shining movement. Why, there's something absolutely gorgeous over there! She must move closer so she can discern this newest wonder of the garden. She will, of course, just look—and then she'll hurry back to Adam. What fun it may be to tell him of her adventure. She creeps forward. She is determined not to venture nearer than just enough to get a closer look. Ever so slowly she covers the intervening distance . . . until she reaches the edge of a small open space. Eve stands stock still, gazing at the most beautiful being she has ever beheld. Adam, of course, is glorious in his own right. But this . . . the color, the stature, the innate gracefulness of the figure leaning there against the tree trunk takes her breath away.

Into the bird song and the gentle rustle of Eden's never-browning foliage comes a subtle, sibilant voice. Why, this . . . this wondrous being is speaking! Speaking to her! He pronounces her name; there's music in the voice. He gestures toward the tree limbs over his head. Her eyes follow. The fruit seems unlike that anywhere else in the garden; it glistens in the sunlight as a gentle breeze rustles the leaves. Eve's mouth waters. She looks again at the glowing personality before her. He takes a step toward her. Uncertainty sweeps over her. Should she leave? But this golden creature is so charming, so attractive. See, he's smiling . . . and beckoning her forward. She moves closer still. Again comes the gesture upward to the branches hanging heavy with fruit. The promised succulence entices Eve more strongly now that she's nearer the tree. The very shape of the individual fruits is intriguing. Their sweet yet tangy aroma assails her nostrils. She shakes her head, seeking to free herself from the fruit's incredible attraction. Again comes the voice of the beautiful creature standing before her. His tone is like a caress—but a caress that awakens rather than calms something within her. Eve feels its effect as a rising flame deep within her breast. Her eyes fasten upon the being's hand as it stretches toward her. It holds a piece of fruit. Shocked to be suddenly so near what she knows is forbidden, she steps backward. But again the voice holds her. The moments pass. Words go back and forth between the woman and the fascinating personality beneath the tree. The fruit itself seems to grow in its attraction; all within Eve unifies into an immense, pulsating core of want. The softly spoken words are all reasonable, compelling. Surely a piece of the tree's product wouldn't . . . couldn't . . . produce death. So she makes her choice. She takes the fruit from the extended hand. She moves it to her mouth. Her teeth sink into the firm, juicy flesh; but as she swallows the sweetness, she ingests the seed of death. The only immediate sensation is something never known before—emptiness in her heart. It marks the yawning grave into which perfection has fallen.

Imagination brought to bear upon scenes in the Bible of course does not necessarily carry weight. Nevertheless, the empty places a woman experiences in her being and in her circumstances do indeed have their origin in Eden and that moment when Eve disobeyed God. Eve didn't need the fruit of the Tree of the Knowledge of Good and Evil. She simply wanted it. Everything since then has been imperfection. Imperfection is incompleteness, shortfall, insufficiency, emptiness. How do you and I experience it in our everyday lives, these long years from Eden?

OUR PERCEPTIONS

Wherever life, others, or self fails to be perfect, we perceive emptiness. As Christians, we know intellectually that our desire for or expectation of perfection in a fallen, sin-marred world is unrealistic. Despite intellectual understanding we experience tremendous struggles as we sense personal empty places. We desire satisfaction—fullness—with every fiber of our being and in every aspect of our existence.

I believe that born-again Christian women generally are more spiritually successful in what we call "big issues" than in those we mistakenly think of as "small" because the latter are personal and intimate. Most of us would vociferously reject such things as an invitation to a bar, an offered hallucinatory drug, proffered involvement in robbing a bank, or sexual allurement by a stranger on the street. Yet we may be defeated when faced with an emotional, relational, or circumstantial emptiness. A "minor" defeat, of course, can be the first step to a greater failure in personal testimony than ever imagined possible. Nor do God's weights and measures coincide with our human ones. The Bible is clear that our heavenly Father judges our "small" internal struggles to be as important, or even more significant, than our public self.

> Thou hast set our iniquities before thee; our secret sins in the light of thy countenance. (Psalm 90:8)

> Keep thy heart with all diligence; for out of it are the issues of life. (Proverbs 4:23)

> He that is slow to anger is better than the mighty; and he that ruleth his spirit than he that taketh a city. (Proverbs 16:32)

We learn in school that nature abhors a vacuum. The same principle applies in the human sense. When we become aware of a personal empty place, we reflexively want to fill it. It's easy to observe how unsaved women do so, and we recognize the harmful results. However, we believers often unwittingly parallel their reactions: we move into self-energized efforts toward fullness. Ultimately, such responses create spiritual negatives that hinder our person and our progress. We play into the hands of our soul's enemy.

Our Opposer

Satan continues to oppose throughout our life just as he battled us at the time of our initial response to Christ's saving gospel. He detests a surrendered, consistent believer, who poses a threat to him through effective prayer God-ward and magnetic ambassadorship man-ward. As the god of this world, Satan uses a full arsenal of spiritual weapons, and he keeps a battery of his guns leveled at our human vulnerabilities. Surely one of the most strategic of those targets is the area labeled "I Need." There you and I lose skirmish after spiritual skirmish. By discounting or denying the importance of such private discomfitures, we weaken our defenses and expose ourselves to the enemy's greater conquest and perhaps even to an ultimate, tragic shattering. Therefore, let's lay aside our self-protective reflexes and side-stepping dishonesties. Let's instead, open ourselves to honest examination of our perceived wants and needs. Our exploratory exercise will be lighted by God's Word.

❦ THINKING IT OVER ❧

Our individualities and intricacies create numberless variations of empty places. That makes it impossible to address each one. However, we can focus upon general categories:

- The mental
- The natural
- The experiential
- The relational

As we explore those places, let's do so with the psalmist's prayer issuing from our heart:

Search me, O God, and know my heart: try me, and know my thoughts: and see if there be any wicked way in me, and lead me in the way everlasting (Psalm 139:23–24).

CHAPTER THREE

MENTAL EMPTINESS

AS THOU KNOWEST NOT WHAT IS THE WAY OF THE SPIRIT,

NOR HOW THE BONES DO GROW IN THE WOMB OF HER THAT

IS WITH CHILD: EVEN SO THOU KNOWEST NOT THE WORKS OF

GOD WHO MAKETH ALL.

ECCLESIASTES 11:5

How soon does any one of us begin to think or say, "I don't understand"? Probably even before we can frame those words. And the phrase is repeated times without number throughout life.

The human mental apparatus shows a facet of God's creative genius that should cause universal amazement and humility. Unsaved mankind, however, insists that the human brain is merely a part of our body that, like every other part, happened into existence and function over a fantastic stretch of time via multitudinous genetic flukes. Since it results from such "natural selection," our mental structure and capacity should be likened to the brains of "other animals." At the same time, unregenerate man determinedly pursues mental understanding of the various aspects of his existence and discounts the reality of that which lies outside his intellectual grasp. What a contradiction! That's like identifying an eland but expecting it to be Einstein!

We who have been made new by the shed blood of Jesus Christ know that the world's conflicting definition of and demands upon our brain are ridiculous, untenable, and God-defying. Yet when we experience winds of intellectual emptiness, we may unintentionally lock ourselves in to mentality's limited resources.

Not understanding the precise workings of a fax machine or the complexities of satellite communication doesn't trouble us overmuch; we simply use them without really comprehending their structure and operation. Our limited mental grasp, however, takes on a more serious cast when we face challenging questions by unbelievers or inexplicable personal experiences. Consider some examples.

While there are some people of both genders who thrive on debate, probably most women do not. Thus, tough questions posed by unbelievers can move us to near panic. Some questions arise repeatedly:

- Why human hatreds, cruelties, and atrocities?
- Why is there the awfulness of war?
- How can a good God let evil triumph?
- If there really is a loving God, why does He allow people to suffer?
- What about individuals born with handicaps?

Listening to those and similar challenges, we hear, as it were, winds screaming of our intellectual insufficiency—we can produce no satisfactory answers to such enormous queries.

When an unsaved person questions God's existence or His character, we somehow feel personally responsible to explain His being and justify His dealings. We defensively attempt to offer answers, however tenuous they may be. Such an encounter proves unsatisfactory, and we heap blame upon ourselves for having been inadequate to meet the challenge.

Intellectual empty places of this sort are essentially self-created: we set out to explain that which is inexplicable. A god who can be understood is no god at all. Challenges to the Lord Jehovah and His dealings are laughable effrontery. When faced with mocking questions, a believer is wise to activate Ecclesiastes 5:2—

> Be not rash with thy mouth, and let not thine heart be hasty to utter any thing before God: for God is in heaven, and thou upon earth: therefore let thy words be few.

That reminder of the vast distance between heaven and earth can curb our frail attempt to bridge the unbridgeable.

Too, consider the challenger. An unsaved questioner or a Christian seeking an excuse for sinfulness is by biblical definition a fool. Consider the interesting, detailed character sketch God gives of fools:

> The fool hath said in his heart, There is no god. (Psalm 14:1)

> Fools despise wisdom and instruction. (Proverbs 1:7)

> The wise in heart will receive commandments; but a prating fool shall fall. (Proverbs 10:8)

> The way of a fool is right in his own eyes. (Proverbs 12:15)

> Fools die for want of wisdom. (Proverbs 10:21)

> The heart of fools proclaimeth foolishness. (Proverbs 12:23)

> A fool layeth open his [own] folly. (Proverbs 13:16)

> It is abomination to fools to depart from evil. (Proverbs 13:19)

> Fools make a mock at sin. (Proverbs 14:9)

> The fool rageth, and is confident. (Proverbs 14:16)

> The mouth of fools poureth out foolishness. (Proverbs 15:2)

The mouth of fools feedeth on foolishness. (Proverbs 15:14)

Folly is joy to him that is destitute of wisdom. (Proverbs 15:2)

A fool's lips enter into contention, and his mouth calleth for strokes. (Proverbs 18:6)

A fool's mouth is his destruction, and his lips are the snare of his soul. (Proverbs 18:7)

Wisdom is too high for a fool. (Proverbs 24:7)

Not only does God define the fool; He also instructs us to be wise in responding to such a person:

Answer not a fool according to his folly, lest thou also be like unto him. Answer a fool according to his folly, lest he be wise in his own conceit. (Proverbs 26:4–5)

A fool uttereth all his mind, but a wise man keepeth it in till afterwards. (Proverbs 29:11)

Seest thou a man that is hasty in his words? there is more hope of a fool than of him. (Proverbs 29:20)

The questioner's motivation is either defensive or combative; he or she won't be satisfied by any answer. Feeling that we must speak in God's defense actually may work contrary to the desired effect. That is, unenlightened by the Word of God and the Holy Spirit, an unsaved arguer will advance challenge after challenge, relying entirely upon human reason. She is unable to pass its boundaries herself, and our resort to that which lies beyond—in the realm of faith—merely angers and frustrates her. She will concentrate so fully upon her own logical demands that she'll claim victory and leave the encounter feeling triumphant.

How much better it is to maintain internal quietness engendered by Scripture:

The fear of the Lord is the beginning of wisdom, and the knowledge of the holy is understanding. (Proverbs 9:10)

The secret things belong unto the Lord our God; but those things which are revealed belong unto us and to our children for ever, that we may do all the words of this law. (Deuteronomy 29:29)

O the depth of the riches both of the wisdom and knowledge of God! how unsearchable are his judgments, and his ways past finding out! (Romans 11:33)

Jesus' dealing with the woman of Samaria (John 4) is instructive for us in our own challenging encounters. The woman whom Jesus met there at the well was argumentative at several points. She sought answers and was persistent in her mental probing. Jesus, however, just as persistently responded with a spiritual focus, and He used a minimal number of words. He didn't argue or explain; rather, He addressed her soul's questing. Then He presented His own unique ability to meet her real need.

God is wholly beyond our defense for either His being or His actions. In an unsaved person's questions we need to hear—as Jesus did there at the well-side—not intellectual exercise but spiritual emptiness. Turning queries back upon the questioner can lead her to admit that her own daily existence includes numberless things she does not understand but nevertheless trusts—or to which she entrusts herself. Whether it be the missing "proofs" of evolution's theory or the mysteries of gravity, electricity, or a fax machine, she regularly demonstrates faith. Perhaps the simplest, most classic illustration is that of a chair. She sits on a chair many times in any one day of life. Yet doing so demonstrates faith—trust that the chair will hold her weight. If the woman to whom we're speaking must acknowledge faith's operation in ordinary things of life, one blockade has been minimized or removed. That may prove to be the point at which we can give a personal testimony and begin a presentation of the gospel.

Why this caution against intellectual argumentation? Debate may be effective in a strictly formal, political, or educational setting, but it has little positive benefit spiritually because debate is antagonistic in nature. Our life purpose as Christians is to be magnetic. Intellectual dueling leaves the heart cold; compassionate probing addresses the heart's vulnerability and entices it toward Truth.

> But foolish and unlearned questions avoid, knowing that they do render strifes. And the servant of the Lord must not strive, but be gentle unto all men, apt to teach, patient, in meekness instructing those that oppose themselves; if God peradventure will give them repentance to the acknowledging of the truth. (II Timothy 2:23–25)

Ultimately, then, in situations of intellectual challenge, we experience an empty place—all unnecessarily—when we reach for our own puny mental fencing foil instead of God's mighty sword.

PERSONAL CHALLENGES

While we may seldom face tough questioning by others like those described, we will inevitably have to do so within ourselves. Life's universal complexities eventually touch each of us. Our personal mental wrestling matches can either shake or strengthen our faith. When the towering uncertainties inherent in human existence invade our own life, generalities become painful specifics. Let's think through some examples.

- ~ How can human evil be so pervasive that a murderer's hand strikes my mother?
- ~ Why such hatreds as that which turns my next-door neighbor against me?

- Why must war sabers rattle to such a degree that my son is wounded or killed in military service?
- How can it be that my best friend is blinded and disfigured by a fiery auto collision?
- How can my child be born with a physical or mental handicap?
- Why should my sweet spiritual mentor live out her latter days in a painful, wasting disease?
- How could my husband proclaim himself to be a homosexual and die of AIDS?

When we experience such situations, multiple strands of shock, disillusionment, helpless anger, heart pain, and difficult adjustments twist together into a tightening noose that threatens our spiritual breath. We gasp out that pathetic query "Why?" The wind within the word's utterance itself screams of our empty understanding.

Why, indeed. Were we to ask that question each day of our earthly life, letting it drive us to every published or spoken human source, we could never find satisfaction. Such things lie beyond the capacity of human brain cells: they truly are intellectual empty places.

As Christians, our only wise recourse is to turn from intellectual leaning and toward spiritual learning. We are urged to do that in one of our most oft-quoted Scripture passages, Proverbs 3:5–6—

> Trust in the Lord with all thine heart, and lean not unto thine own understanding. In all thy ways acknowledge him, and he shall direct thy paths.

When we disobey that instruction and lean toward intellectual supply, our leaning gets us off-balance, setting us up for Satan's shove toward disaster. Don't we frequently see demonstrations of that sad scenario? Several within my own circle of acquaintances come to mind. Let me paint two composite pictures of leaning instead of learning.

A girl we'll call Jill responds in childhood to the gospel presentation at a neighborhood VBS. Following her salvation, she continues to attend the theologically liberal, culturally compromising church in which her parents are members. Following the urging of the woman who led her to the Lord, Jill spends time daily reading her Bible; she experiences conflict as she recognizes the difference between what she reads and what she sees and hears at her church.

After high school graduation she enrolls in a local junior college. There she sits in the classes of atheistic teachers who take every opportunity to mock Christianity. During those same two years her parents' marriage shatters, and her mother commits suicide. Shaken by the intense intellectual, emotional, and spiritual bombardment and recognizing herself to be ill-equipped with Scripture knowledge, she decides to transfer to a Christian college to complete her degree. She mentally scripts a dream that grows to theater-screen proportions: she will go to the Christian college, escape the sorrow of her personal losses and the frustrations of ungodly public education, meet the man of her dreams, and live happily ever after.

The Christian college does surround her with the encouraging warmth of its spiritual atmosphere, godly teaching, and positive relationships, but because of her loosely disciplined background she chafes under campus rules. She meets a student—Jim—who, like she, stands apart from wholehearted, receptive involvement. Jim resents the school's spiritual emphasis, and he sails as close as possible to the outer edge of acceptability. In their conversations he persistently but subtly leads Jill into questioning God's goodness in allowing her parents' divorce and her mother's death. He also reminds her of the "intellectually honest" assertions made by her teachers in the junior college. He admires and accepts humanistic pronouncements as more tenable than Christianity's opposing position. While he protests his "basic" agreement with Scripture, he constantly reads and quotes from unsaved writers. Jim's personal magnetism and self-advertised intellectual powers pull bricks out of Jill's shaky spiritual structure. Her freewheeling father approves of Jim and his ideas.

Pressured by what she considers to be their superior intellects, Jill abandons her spiritual quest in favor of "rationality." She marries Jim after they graduate from college. The wedding takes place in her liberal home church. Soon even that nondemanding religious affiliation becomes burdensome; the young couple chooses cultural conformity and plunges into the secular life stream. Pursuit of the American dream becomes their entire existence.

Another couple, the Smiths, a godly ministry couple, faithfully work and pray to bring their children up in the nurture and admonition of the Lord. When the children reach adulthood, however, tragedy strikes not once but twice. Their daughter marries a man who proves to be a wife-beater within his home and a crooked businessman outside it. He seeks a divorce, leaving her with three small children. Their son likewise enters a disastrous marriage to a woman who walks out on him after committing multiple adulteries. Brokenhearted, the young man turns to alcohol and drugs. As the ministry parents helplessly watch their children's lives disintegrate, they search for understanding. They examine their child-rearing efforts, the home atmosphere they created, their persistent prayer efforts, the balance they sought to maintain between the ministry demands and their parenting. When they can find nothing to throw the light of comprehension into their sorrow-darkened minds, they slowly loosen their grip upon things formerly held as essential.

Embarrassed by actual or supposed criticism from those with whom they've been associated for years, they seek new friendship circles where life standards are less scriptural and more "practical." They begin to tolerate things in their ministry heretofore eschewed, including rock music and immodest dress. They compromise the message of the Bible in the pulpit, youth group, Sunday school classes, and the women's ministry, ultimately interpreting Christian liberty as "anything goes with God." Enjoying increased income from the more affluent congregation attracted by the changes, they take on a patina of glamour. They invest money, attention, and time on self-improvement and upscale socializing.

How could such personal and ministry declension happen? Both began with an intellectual empty place: incomprehension. Something must fill that void. A mind unable to discern meaning in painful experiences stands at a point of choice. The options, really, are only two: self or the Savior. Self, as it were, folds its arms protectively around its mental frustration and capitulates to emotion. Though we know that either rebellion or collapse is unworthy of Christianity, the struggle for genuine submission can be intense and prolonged. In many cases, too, we worsen the internal warfare by keeping it hidden. Unless we ultimately stop leaning toward our own understanding and instead seek to learn lessons of faith, incomprehension fosters emotional redirection: we move away from the sovereign God rather than toward Him.

Leaning toward our own understanding can also tip us toward intellectual competition. Argumentative challenges, worldly disparagement of Bible-based thinking, or incomprehensible personal circumstances can motivate a person to pursue mental enhancement for its own sake. Each of us, of course, has the stewardship responsibility to develop our individual mental capabilities. We should neither waste nor worship our mind. Expanding human knowledge as an end in itself is not only chasing something of little worth but can be deeply dangerous in the spiritual sense.

Unnumbered seekers of intellectual achievement end by worshiping a false god—the idol of intellect.

At one point in my life I found myself among such intellectual idolators. While working toward a master's degree, my husband and I took some upper-level courses at a prestigious state university in the north. When the summer sessions began, I was cowed by the superior airs and self-conscious verbiage of our fellow students. Before long, though, the truth of the situation became apparent: the supercilious aura and polysyllabic word choices were merely the trappings of intellect worship. Time, tests, and performance revealed that behind the trappings lay shallow mental reality. Too, the lack of soul depth was unmistakable in their words, attitudes, and actions. Nevertheless, the professors consistently modeled and encouraged the intellectual façade. Solomon long ago warned against that kind of scholastic pursuit:

> Cease, my son, to hear the instruction that causeth thee to err from the words of knowledge. (Proverbs 19:27)

Probably each of us is acquainted with a "lifetime student"—a person who finds no satisfaction in a college degree, a master's degree, or even a doctorate, but rather continues along one or more scholastic pathways years without end. Such a pursuit obviously shifts emphasis away from the faithful, balanced practicality of wise living God tells us to have. It also actually expands intellectual frustration, because the more we learn in any field, the more we realize how much there is yet to learn! The whole can never be absorbed.

Fruitless pursuits of earthly knowledge—our own understanding—are rebuked by Ecclesiastes 1:18—

> For in much wisdom is much grief; and he that increaseth knowledge increaseth sorrow.

The human mind is marvelous in its abilities, and as stewards of our intellectual gifts we Christians should take advantage of and work diligently in every educational opportunity the Lord gives us. It is shameful not to do so. It's also lazily dishonest to claim that inferior education equals superior spirituality.

For the believer, however, stewardship of our mental faculties extends beyond IQ and cognitive skills. Besides intellectual gifting, God also gives to His born-again ones the capacity to gain spiritual wisdom. That is the learning we should most earnestly pursue. Such learning involves the whole internal person—the soul and spirit as well as the mind.

> Also, that the soul be without knowledge, it is not good. (Proverbs 19:2)

The wise soul understands that incisive human thinking or eloquent words can't effectively silence the gainsayers of this world or plumb the mysteries of human existence. It also knows that divinity is neither threatened nor thwarted by His creatures. God sits in serene sovereignty, holding unregenerate man's railings against Him in derision. His eternal truth is as the boundless universe through which our tiny, separate planets of mortal understanding orbit. Isn't it amazing that such specks of intellectual dust consider themselves sufficient to question, challenge, and rail against His limitless, sustaining expanse? Faith's wisdom recognizes the divine universe and honors it; human mentality sees no further than its own dust mote.

Rather than rue intellectual insufficiencies, we can instead rest upon the all-knowing mind of God and rejoice in the sure knowledge that however His works may puzzle us, they are "true and righteous altogether" (Psalm 19:9). Such resting, however, doesn't mean that we're content with our spiritual IQ. God tells us how, what, and why to study:

> Study to show thyself approved unto God, a workman that needeth not to be ashamed, rightly dividing the word of truth. But shun profane and vain babblings: for they will increase unto more ungodliness. (II Timothy 2:15–16)

We each need to soak in God's Word, expanding our soul as well as our mind in order to respond rightly when we face queries or puzzling circumstances. The expansion produced by such soaking will lead us to put aside our words in favor of God's Word. When we don't use the Bible effectively in our human contacts, we reveal some unlovely things:

- We don't have sufficient knowledge of the Word to use it.
- We don't trust the Word for sufficiency.
- We consider our mind equal to whatever challenge is at hand.

Soul wisdom is not only aware of II Timothy 3:16–17; it also consistently applies the passage:

> All scripture is given by inspiration of God, and is profitable for doctrine, for reproof, for correction, for instruction in righteousness: that the man of God may be perfect, throughly furnished unto all good works.

Even a new Christian can quote the verse as a means of establishing or emphasizing the doctrine of biblical inspiration. But it's a rare believer who actually uses the inspired Word for her own spiritual reproof, correction, and instruction. No wonder so few of us are perfect (mature), thoroughly prepared for and effectively engaged in the good works God desires in us. One such "good work" is confronting human error with God's truth.

The person who questions God's existence or His equity may heartily dislike Bible quotation and deny its applicability, expressing intense dissatisfaction or anger when we stick to Bible responses.

So be it. What greater, better authority can we possibly cite? Just as human argumentation leans heavily on the opinion of respected authority, so the believer relies upon divine revelation. Just as the other person is free to choose intellectual argumentation, so we have the right to choose divine proclamation. When the questioner throws out evolutionary "expert" sources, we can quietly quote Jeremiah 51:15—

> He hath made the earth by his power, he hath established the world by his wisdom, and hath stretched out the heaven by his understanding.

Suppose the person with whom you're conversing throws up the old line "How could a good God let someone be born blind, deaf, or crippled?" Rather than attempting an explanation of the Creator, a Scripture exaltation of Him can be effective.

> The hearing ear, and the seeing eye, the Lord hath made even both of them. (Proverbs 20:12)

Although that response stays within the area of the questioner's focus, it comes from the opposite direction and extols marvels that she must admit, even if only in the scientific or structural sense.

In confrontational situations, we naturally concentrate our attention and effort on the product of our lips—words. The product of our heart is equally important—our spirit. Let's think again how Scripture states the imperatives.

> But the wisdom that is from above is first pure, then peaceable, gentle, and easy to be intreated, full of mercy and good fruits, without partiality, and without hypocrisy. (James 3:17)

> And the servant of the Lord must not strive, but be gentle unto all men, apt to teach, patient, in meekness instructing those that oppose themselves. (II Timothy 2:24–25)

> But sanctify the Lord God in your hearts: and be ready always to
> give an answer to every man that asketh you a reason of the hope
> that is in you with meekness and fear. (I Peter 3:15)

Tension over our intellectual limitations can make us seem
angry or self-righteous. Genuine reliance upon God's limitless wisdom creates meekness and gentleness. In other words, faith must
step in to fill our cerebral empty places and to clothe our spirit in
humility. Winning an argument is not important; rightly represent-
ing Jesus Christ is.

We will do well to remember the immense difference between
an unregenerate mind and a Christian's mind. In writing to believers at Ephesus, Paul pointed out that distinction.

> This I say therefore, and testify in the Lord, that ye henceforth
> walk not as other Gentiles walk, in the vanity of their mind,
> having the understanding darkened, being alienated from the
> life of God through the ignorance that is in them, because of the
> blindness of their heart. (Ephesians 4:17–18)

In writing to Titus, the apostle Paul gave valuable instruction
about dealing with those of opposing beliefs.

> In all things showing thyself a pattern of good works: in doctrine
> showing uncorruptness, gravity, sincerity, sound speech, that
> cannot be condemned; that he that is of the contrary part may
> be ashamed, having no evil thing to say of you. (Titus 2:7–8)

Our encounters with people who express antagonism toward
God may be infrequent; our own wrestling matches with life's mysteries are more often experienced. The human mind craves to understand, and when it encounters impenetrable matters, its natural
tendency is to balk and object, to argue and resent.

Blessed is that person who from childhood is taught that there
are more things in life lying beyond our understanding than within

it. Thus, she is somewhat equipped to deal with earth's puzzles. Even more blessed is that person who from early childhood has Christian parents teaching and demonstrating that our God is loving, sovereign, omniscient, righteous, and good in Himself and in all His doings. As she walks on in her personal relationship with Jesus Christ, though she will struggle when confronted by unknowables, her training will lessen the battle's intensity, shorten its length, and encourage her positive adjustment.

Whatever our home training may have been, however, our Father's great instruction book powerfully points the way to God-pleasing mental operation.

THINKING IT OVER

Puzzling places in life should motivate us to rely upon God and to monitor our responses. Proverbs 16:1–3 is applicable:

> The preparations of the heart in man, and the answer of the tongue, is from the Lord. All the ways of a man are clean in his own eyes: but the Lord weigheth the spirits. Commit thy works unto the Lord, and thy thoughts shall be established.

CHAPTER FOUR

REMEASURING MENTAL EMPTINESS

BE NOT HASTY IN THY SPIRIT TO BE ANGRY; FOR ANGER REST-
ETH IN THE BOSOM OF FOOLS. SAY NOT THOU, WHAT IS THE
CAUSE THAT THE FORMER DAYS WERE BETTER THAN THESE?
FOR THOU DOST NOT INQUIRE WISELY CONCERNING THIS.

ECCLESIASTES 7:9–10

Acknowledging our mental insufficiency can launch us toward
God's Word when life presents puzzles.

The eternal I AM rebukes our intellectual frustrations, telling
us of His mind and its immeasurable superiority to ours. Let's go to
a few passages that help redirect our reliance from humanity's intellectual poverty to divinity's wealth of wisdom.

Ecclesiastes 2:13 tells us why we should pursue godly wisdom.

Then I saw that wisdom excelleth folly, as far as light excelleth
darkness.

What, then, can be our first step in the right direction? Isaiah
8:13 is an effective steppingstone.

> Sanctify [or "hallow"] the Lord of hosts himself; and let him be
> your fear, and let him be your dread.

That verse actually provides a kneeling stone even more than a steppingstone, doesn't it? A kneeling heart—submissive and seeking—is the essential first response for every aspect of successful Christian living.

Reading and studying the Old Testament makes us stand amazed at the great minds so evident on its pages—minds that display not only high human intelligence but also transcendent spiritual wisdom. The prophet Isaiah is certainly one of those. That fiery Old Testament prophet did not spring spiritually full grown into being God's effective servant. The Lord allows us to witness at least part of his transformation: we might call it a moment spent on a kneeling stone. Tracing the incident offers us priceless personal enlightenment.

The opening verse of Isaiah 6 gives the setting:

> In the year that king Uzziah died, I saw also the Lord sitting
> upon a throne, high and lifted up, and his train filled the
> temple.

The phrase "In the year that king Uzziah died" connects strongly to our theme of emptiness. Standing alone, the phrase has little or no significance. But when we look into the historical era, the text takes on power.

The Old Testament listing of Israel's and Judah's kings contains forthright evaluations:

- "He did that which was evil in the sight of the Lord."
- "He did that which was right."

Second Chronicles 26 traces the reign of King Uzziah. He came to the throne of Judah following the death of his father, Amaziah. He was only sixteen years old at the time. He reigned fifty-two years, and most of that reign was spiritually positive. As Scripture records, "And he did that which was right in the sight of the Lord" (II Chronicles 26:4).

Just as in our day, so it was then as well: there were far more wicked rulers than good ones. When a ruler did wickedly his influence permeated society, and those who remained true to Jehovah suffered. Thus, worshipers of the Lord Jehovah would have valued the unusual and lengthy period of spiritual good under Uzziah.

Now focus again on the phrase "In the year that king Uzziah died." Uzziah had been the human source of Isaiah's freedom to live for and preach Jehovah. The king's death, therefore, would have made a powerful impact upon Isaiah, who was as thoroughly human as you and I are. No doubt there was regret over the end of an era and unease over what might follow. The heir apparent, Jotham, had poor character and questionable faith. In other words, Isaiah would have experienced the emptiness of uncertainties.

Now come to the next phrases in the passage, still keeping in mind the importance of the timing: "I saw also the Lord sitting upon a throne, high and lifted up, and his train filled the temple."

The prophet's uneasy horizontal focus was abruptly arrested and redirected, as we see in verse 5. Instantly, there was shrinkage of self and of earthly concerns in that moment as Isaiah cried out: "Woe is me! for I am undone: because I am a man of unclean lips."

Do you imagine that scene with Isaiah standing upright in the presence of God? I don't. The prophet's legs must have given way, causing him to fall to his knees. What was it that swept his earlier concerns into oblivion? Isaiah himself tells us, as his heart continues its cry: "Mine eyes have seen the King, the Lord of hosts."

God didn't point to any earthly or human reassurance; instead, He allowed a vision of Himself. The sight completely and gloriously filled Isaiah's intellectual empty place. From his position there on the kneeling stone, the prophet yielded himself to move forward however Jehovah should command.

Then said I, Here am I, send me. (6:8)

Isaiah's experience in that moment so long ago can challenge us to turn from our own mind's muddles to God's eternal truths. Wherever and whenever our understanding produces an empty place, we're to put aside our own surmising and honor God by bowing our hearts before Him, waiting for Him to work according to His will.

God allowed Isaiah a single vision of Himself. He graciously gives you and me a constantly available vision throughout the Bible. Scripture's revelation of God is far more extensive and personal than was His one-time appearance to Isaiah. Yet we fail to seek and see Him there as we ought. That failure marks the crucial point from which we depart into our own minuscule mental resources.

While many places in Scripture help us to bow our hearts before the Lord of Hosts, none does so more majestically than Isaiah 40.

> Who hath measured the waters in the hollow of his hand, and meted out heaven with the span, and comprehended the dust of the earth in a measure, and weighed the mountains in scales, and the hills in a balance? Who hath directed the Spirit of the Lord, or being his counselor hath taught him? With whom took he counsel, and who instructed him, and taught him knowledge, and shewed to him the way of understanding? . . . All nations before him are as nothing; and they are counted to him less than nothing, and vanity. . . . It is he that sitteth upon the circle of the earth, and the inhabitants thereof are as grasshoppers; that stretcheth out the heavens as a curtain, and spreadeth them out as a tent to dwell in. That bringeth the princes to nothing; he maketh the judges of the earth as vanity. . . . To whom then will ye liken me, or shall I be equal? saith the Holy One. Lift up your

eyes on high, and behold who hath created these things, that
bringeth out their host by number: he calleth them all by names
by the greatness of his might, for that he is strong in power; not
one faileth. (Isaiah 40:12–14, 17, 22–23, 25–26)

When faced with any intellectual empty place, we can flee to
that Mighty One in Whom resides the wisdom of all eternity. Nor
does He remain aloof in His unlimited wisdom: He offers—yea,
graciously promises—to extend that wisdom to you and me! King
Solomon reminds us,

> For the Lord giveth wisdom; out of his mouth cometh knowledge
> and understanding (Proverbs 2:6).

And what Christian has not thrilled at God's pronouncement as
recorded in Jeremiah 33:3?

> Call unto me, and I will answer thee, and show thee great and
> mighty things which thou knowest not.

God spoke that promise to Jeremiah when he was a prisoner.
The prophet's situation wasn't desired or deserved, and his comprehension of it undoubtedly came up short. The circumstances
seemed to signal triumph of wrong and defeat of right. But while
Jeremiah's perception may have been mired, Jehovah's purpose and
power were transcendent.

The New Testament, too, urges us toward active faith in puzzling times. The book of James is powerfully practical. In fact, it's
sometimes called the Proverbs of the New Testament. It opens with
the writer's salutation to scattered, beleaguered believers. Recognizing that their experiences were challenging their understanding,
the Holy Spirit moved James to write,

> If any of you lack wisdom, let him ask of God, that giveth to
> all men liberally, and upbraideth not; and it shall be given him
> (James 1:5).

It's often true that things most familiar are things most disregarded. People who live near a tourist attraction may be the least likely to visit the site. I believe this principle works persistently in Christians with regard to Scripture. Familiarity with various passages can act as a barrier to our accessing the riches of those passages. That being the case, let's examine together how we might use James 1:5 as an antidote to our ever-plaguing mental empty places. We'll do so by applying the verse itself phrase by phrase.

If any of you lack wisdom . . .

To experience the wonderful reality of this promise, we must operate upon its premise. In other words, we must personally recognize our mental insufficiency. That demands both honesty and humility. Whether aloud or silently, we have to say in effect, "Dear Father, my brain can't handle this. I can't think of a fitting response to her challenge . . . This experience lies beyond explanation . . . Lord, my pain puts my mind into deep freeze." How much farther along the path to spiritual maturity you and I would be if our first response to intellectual emptiness were to turn God-ward! Much more typically, however, it's our very belated response, isn't it? We spend—and waste—so much time and emotional energy scrambling madly down labyrinthine corridors of our mind, only to find that none of them leads to the supply we need. Instead, we should be quick to admit that we lack wisdom—period!

Let him ask of God . . .

Petitioning our heavenly Father should be the immediate outgrowth of our confessed emptiness. But no matter how long we've been saved, the tendency toward self-help maintains a strong grip on our mental apparatus. We "ask" more urgently of our own intellectual storehouse, agitatedly feeling the answers must be tucked away in there someplace. Or we run to our bookshelves, racking our memory for an appropriate statement once read. Or we reach for the telephone to call someone who might be able to help us. Why do we jump up off our knees where we've just admitted our insufficiency? Rather than looking within or around, God wants us to turn our soul's eyes upward and seek His mind.

As James 1:5 goes on, it's as if God wants to underline the individuality as well as the inclusiveness of His promise. First, there was "any of you." Now He doubles back for emphasis:

That giveth to all men liberally, and upbraideth not . . .

What a beautiful, encouraging phrase for even the most intense intellectual need. Note the inclusiveness of God's accessible wisdom. He gives to any of us: "all men." There's no prerequisite stage, age, or station. I've had many occasions to rejoice and wonder at this reality. As women have quietly shared with me their experiences of understanding's shortfall and God's supply of wisdom in tough, trying situations, my heart could only pay tribute to their faith. Through His promised, gracious bestowment the most unlikely and unrecognized Christian women soar to heights of wisdom that put many a full-time Christian worker to shame. Just so does our great God give of His wisdom to those who seek Him.

His giving is unstinting as well. His mighty heart's overflowing love reflects into magnanimous supply of wisdom for His children. Clearly, then, any of my barely-enough-to-squeeze-by "smarts" result from my failure to ask for and activate His liberal supply!

The closing words reach out to hug us:

And upbraideth not.

Our wonderful God doesn't fuss at us for our determined foolishness. Do we deserve to be scolded? Absolutely! The older I get, the more utterly amazed I am that my Father puts up with me. My stupidities and failures far surpass any wise moments and victories.

In fact, they don't just surpass; they eclipse them. But the tender, tender heart of God always responds to His child's plea with patience and love. I know full well I should hear, "All right, Dummy, though you've blown it yet again, I'll trust you with a few crumbs." But no—instead comes the silent, soul-warming response of the divine heart: "Beloved Dummy, hold up your battered little cup; I'll pour and pour until it overflows."

And finally comes the promise:

And it shall be given him.

James 1:5, of course, does not stand isolated from the surrounding text. Verses 6–7 tell us our part in the transaction. We're to ask believing. God wants our belief to be simple and childlike—God said it. I believe it. I'll act upon it.

Only then will we know God's supply of wisdom.

There are times when, while actively seeking wisdom from the Lord, we should also avail ourselves of human counsel:

Blessed is the man that walketh not in the counsel of the ungodly. (Psalm 1:1)

Where no counsel is, the people fall: but in the multitude of counselors there is safety. (Proverbs 11:14)

He that hearkeneth unto counsel is wise. (Proverbs 12:15)

Any counselor should be chosen with great care, and the advice he or she gives must always be prayerfully compared with Scripture.

The counsel of the Lord standeth for ever, the thoughts of his heart to all generations. (Psalm 33:11)

There are many devices in a man's heart; nevertheless the counsel of the Lord, that shall stand. (Proverbs 19:21)

Wisdom is a critical need not only as we seek and receive counsel but also when we are asked to give it. Most of us at one time or another will be approached by a person seeking advice. Anyone called upon for counsel faces a tremendous responsibility. We would do well to remember—and be warned by—God's strong denunciation of the "help" offered to the suffering Job by his friends.

> Who is this that darkeneth counsel by words without knowledge?
> (Job 38:2)

One of the most disheartening things I encounter on the Christian scene today is the giving of "faux pearls" in counsel. The old term "pearls of wisdom" certainly can be applied to the Bible's own counsel, as it also can be to Bible-anchored, prayerfully presented human advice. But knee-jerk responses from a counselor are faux pearls. Many confused, hurting individuals bring their agonized queries to someone of reputation or position, only to be given shoot-from-the-hip, one-size-fits-all, paint-by-number answers or advice. What a regrettable disservice! Such careless responses to difficult questions recall the solemn pronouncement of Psalm 94:11:

> The Lord knoweth the thoughts of man, that they are vanity.

In a college class called Women in Christian Service, another teacher and I not only encourage the students' questions during and after each lecture but also end every semester of instruction with two full class periods given to questions the girls submit anonymously. As you might imagine, every open forum invites intense, specific probing by these young women who are approaching their college graduation. Through the years of standing before these who are so precious to my heart, I've seen their questions reflect the world's worsening condition: they touch upon situations, actions, attitudes, and experiences we of earlier generations never had to face. It is disheartening to realize that these young women—most of whom are from Christian homes and good churches—have had critical areas of need either left unaddressed or unsatisfactorily answered. The only honest, adequate response for many of their questions is to point out that there is no fixed answer. Sinful society's ever-worsening declension has so compromised individuals, so contaminated relationships, and so complicated life circumstances that problems demand the Christian diligently seek God's own enlightenment and intervention.

A knee-jerk response is too often given by a counselor because he or she doesn't want to appear inadequate by saying, "I don't know." Therein lies the ultimate reason for much misinformation and misdirection: the counselor's pride.

While there are general principles and nonspecific Scripture indications to apply in even the toughest situations brought to a counselor, precise answers can be found only as the involved individuals search the written Word and earnestly petition the Living Word. Thereby they'll receive genuine pearls of wisdom.

The term "pearls of wisdom" can help direct each of us toward proper evaluation and pursuit of that precious commodity. Manmade pearls may appear attractive and costly; but under the thin veneer there's only a valueless form. Genuine pearls, on the other hand, are rare, precious, and obtained through great determination and diligence. Proverbs 2 challenges us to pursue godly wisdom with similar single-mindedness:

> My son, if thou wilt receive my words, and hide my commandments with thee; so that thou incline thine ear unto wisdom, and apply thine heart to understanding; yea, if thou criest after knowledge and liftest up thy voice for understanding; if thou seekest her as silver, and searchest for her as for hid treasures; then shalt thou understand the fear of the Lord, and find the knowledge of God (verses 1–5).

Proverbs 8 further extols wisdom, doing so in the form of a wonderful personification. Verse 21 tells us of her "pearlized" antidote for intellectual emptiness:

> That I may cause those that love me to inherit substance: and I will fill their treasures.

If our mental supply is scanty, it's because we've not diligently plumbed its limitless resource, the Word of God. Proverbs 22:20–21 speaks with unmistakable clarity:

> Have not I written to thee excellent things in counsels and knowledge, that I might make thee know the certainty of the words of truth; that thou mightest answer the words of truth to them that send unto thee?

In the New Testament, too, godly wisdom is contrasted with human understanding. The identification marks of wisdom are given in James 3:17:

> But the wisdom that is from above is first pure, then peaceable, gentle, and easy to be intreated, full of mercy and good fruits, without partiality and without hypocrisy.

How unlike our own thinking, which so persistently proclaims its flawed substance:

- Sullied rather than pure
- Pettily inflammatory instead of peaceable
- Harsh rather than gentle
- Closed to reasonable entreaty
- Rigid and judgmental instead of merciful
- Barren of spiritual fruit
- Prejudiced rather than impartial
- Insincere instead of genuine

When we lean to our own understanding and fail to seek godly wisdom, we can only be empty intellectually in any sense of eternal importance.

The human brain operates via an electrical and chemical process. In speed, accomplishment, and storage it puts even the most sophisticated computer to shame. Weighing roughly three pounds, the brain is the control center for the entire body. Sometimes the terms "brain" and "mind" are used interchangeably. But they are distinct entities. The *American Heritage Dictionary* defines *mind* as follows:

> The human consciousness that originates in the brain and is manifested especially in thought, perception, emotion, will, memory, and imagination.

Although the human mind cannot be precisely located or its operation analyzed, it's easy to see that in a very real sense it is the control center for our core self—our individual being. While brain and mind are definitely connected, they are just as definitely separate entities. That fact is important to you and me as Christians. We of course need to guard our brain from trauma. Each of us has seen negative results of injured brains, whether the injury resulted from drugs, disease, or blows to the head. Many different body functions can be affected: balance, movement, speech, and so forth. Yet as important as the brain is to physical operation, God doesn't address the brain in His Word—rather, He consistently focuses upon the mind. Let's consider just a few passages.

> For to be carnally minded is death; but to be spiritually minded is life and peace. Because the carnal mind is enmity against God; for it is not subject to the law of God, neither indeed can be. (Romans 8:6–7)

And be not conformed to this world; but be ye transformed by the renewing of your mind, that ye may prove what is that good, and acceptable, and perfect will of God. (Romans 12:2)

For if there be first a willing mind, it is accepted according to that a man hath, and not according to that he hath not. (II Corinthians 8:12)

And be renewed in the spirit of your mind. (Ephesians 4:23)

The brain faithfully drives our physical self without our conscious direction and without our even being aware of its activity. Our mind, however, lies within our control. Think back through the mental aspects given earlier in the dictionary definition:

- Thought
- Perception
- Emotion
- Will
- Memory
- Imagination

Just as the list begins with thought, our every mental response begins there as well. The functioning of that "engine" is under God's constant scrutiny. "Thou understandest my thought afar off" (Psalm 139:2). God nowhere says to us, "Keep your synapses active." He does say, however, that we're to be

bringing into captivity every thought to the obedience of Christ (II Corinthians 10:5).

Thoughts rightly captivated by Jesus Christ through the Word will do the following:

- Evidence Spirit-directed perception
  To know wisdom and instruction; to perceive the words of understanding. (Proverbs 1:2)

- Rule emotional expression
  A foolish woman is clamorous [tumultuous]: she is simple, and knoweth nothing. (Proverbs 9:13)

- Exert will power for godly living
  For I determined not to know any thing among you, save Jesus Christ, and him crucified. (I Corinthians 2:2)

- Relish bright memories and refuse the dark ones
  I will remember the works of the Lord: surely I will remember thy wonders of old. I will meditate also of all thy work, and talk of thy doings. (Psalm 77:11–12)

- Direct the imagination into clear, creative paths
  These six things doth the Lord hate . . . An heart that deviseth wicked imaginations. (Proverbs 6:16, 18)

Clearly, then, the believer's essential with regard to her mind is neither intellect nor education—but Spirit-controlled thinking.

As I wrote this, Bob Jones University lost a longtime faculty member, and the memory of his teaching and testimony brings to my heart a timely illustration.

Dr. Walter Fremont served for many years as the dean of our School of Education. While of course the position demanded a good deal of work in the office, the bulk of his influence came in his teaching and counseling. The most physically dynamic teacher I've ever seen, Dr. Fremont communicated energy and excitement about Christian education—sometimes from atop the teacher's desk. Both in the classroom and in counseling he would take his listeners to God's Word, show them the truth applicable to the situation, and throw out the challenge "Make up your mind! Make up your mind to obey. Make up your mind to do right. Make up your mind!" That challenge was given so consistently and so often that it grated on one's nerves. But he got the point across, and he inspired generations of students to become Christian teachers.

Admonition can be powerful and effective. But another entire dimension of impact is added by demonstration. Dr. Fremont ultimately gave us just such a demonstration. After enduring three years of puzzling symptoms, he was diagnosed with ALS—Lou Gehrig's disease. The physical destruction was irreversible, and it was devastating to watch. But while his body lost function after function, his spirit never lost anything: in fact, it grew stronger and brighter through all of the twenty-plus years before God called him home.

Walter Fremont effectively taught biblical principles. But he even more effectively lived them. His "Make up your mind!" echoed I Peter 1:13—

> Wherefore gird up the loins of your mind, be sober, and hope to the end for the grace that is to be brought unto you at the revelation of Jesus Christ.

THINKING IT OVER

There are many more questions in this life than there are answers. As born-again believers we need to accept the fact of limitations to human comprehension. Whether understanding's shortfall comes in queries and challenges presented by someone else or sets upon us personally in experience, our mental emptiness should draw us to God with increasing awe of His all-knowing mind. Specifically, we can go to Job 38–41. God gives neither reasons nor explanations for the multiple disasters that befell his servant Job, whom God Himself called "a perfect and an upright man, one that feareth God and escheweth evil." The mighty I AM simply presents a sketch of His own transcendent Person. In recognizing that majesty, Job could exclaim,

> Wherefore I abhor myself, and repent in dust and ashes (Job 42:6).

CHAPTER FIVE

Natural Emptiness

I RETURNED, AND SAW UNDER THE SUN, THAT THE RACE IS NOT TO THE SWIFT, NOR THE BATTLE TO THE STRONG, NEITHER YET BREAD TO THE WISE, NOR YET RICHES TO MEN OF UNDERSTANDING, NOR YET FAVOR TO MEN OF SKILL; BUT TIME AND CHANCE HAPPENETH TO THEM ALL.

ECCLESIASTES 9:11

Many Christian women reading the above not only agree with the concept of frailty and vanity but also go past the boundary of sensible actuality into self-denigration, thereby dishonoring our Creator and Savior.

The nagging sense of emptiness is one of life's biggest time and energy wasters. For whatever reason, women are especially conscious and critical of themselves; loath to recognize their gifts, they readily see their lacks.

Personal empty places probably make themselves known most strongly at the time of puberty as girls navigate the difficult transition into womanhood. The winds blowing through this particular cave, however, can also echo into old age.

The unsaved world distorts self-image into an all-important, controlling monstrosity. We as Christians need, instead, to consider our frailty in this area only because of the part it may play in our testimony and service for the Lord. Too often we let our concept of self be a tool in Satan's hands to defeat us and to derail our effectiveness in personal ministry.

While this topic has appeared in my earlier books, it constitutes such a constant, extensive empty place in Christian women that we need to revisit the subject, if only briefly. This is in agreement, I believe, with the Scripture principle of Isaiah 28:10—

> For precept must be upon precept, precept upon precept; line upon line, line upon line; here a little, and there a little.

So let's follow "line upon line" into a few specific caves of natural emptiness wherein we may suffer: body, mind, and emotions.

Women often laugh together about our tendency to dislike ourselves. But behind the lightness of laughter may lurk the heaviness of longing. Not one of us who knows the Lord would be so brazen as to deny that we are—individually and uniquely—created by God, but that doesn't make us pleased with every aspect of His workmanship.

Recently my sister Pat and I were talking on the telephone. Somehow in the midst of our all-too-rare chat, she said "You know, I really always wanted to be tall and slim with long legs—but I'm just a block." All I could do in response was laugh as I remembered how I, on the contrary, had longed to be petite like she is! There it was again—still at our age—reiteration of the wannabes.

Let's consider a few specific areas in which we may typically perceive emptiness.

"I wish" or "I need" or "I don't have" thoughts can quickly surface as we consider our physical body—just as Pat and I experienced jokingly. When we're young, it's hard to withstand the media's high-pressure, glossy selling efforts for having a movie-star face and a model figure. Talk about a manufactured guarantee for unhappiness—that's it! Common sense and spiritual growth ultimately move us beyond those infantile wishes; we accept and adjust to realities of height, weight, and shape. But in their place we may substitute more subtle body-connected dissatisfactions:

- Less-than-tiptop health
- Short supply of physical strength
- Low natural vitality
- Decreasing stamina

Such physical states impose real limitations, but the important thing is our response to the reality. Our natural reaction is to complain about the condition, use it as an excuse, or advertise it as a ploy for attention and sympathy.

We need to acknowledge two things if, instead, we're to respond rightly to the intricacies of our physical structure and functioning. First, we need to remind ourselves that our viewpoint is inevitably faulty in some particular. Therefore, we must seek God's perspective—which is always spiritual. Psalm 119:137 says it well:

Righteous art thou, O Lord, and upright are thy judgments.

Obviously, such a God merits my trust that He has done, is doing, and will continue to do all that is right in and for my physical self.

Second, from that foundational acknowledgement we can move on to Psalm 119:73—

Thy hands have made me and fashioned me: give me understanding, that I may learn thy commandments.

The psalmist's first phrase bespeaks wonderful, settled acceptance of himself physically. From that he moves on to petition his Creator's instruction for proper living within the body given him. The Scripture's joining of physical construction and spiritual instruction should challenge each of us. Let's now apply that concept to the specific personal concerns mentioned earlier.

PHYSICAL LIMITATIONS

Frustration with our physical resources focuses on the fact that they limit our activities, involvements, and accomplishments. Such frustration, however, indicates that at least to some degree our life pursuits are self-defined. Proverbs 16:9 addresses that all-too-common mindset:

> A man's heart deviseth his way: but the Lord directeth his steps.

Surely one of the strongest, most constantly active tendencies of the human heart is that of creating plans according to its own desires. Picture, for instance, a group of girls talking together. If the topic of the future comes up, each one chips in: "I want to be a missionary to Bangladesh." "I'm going to travel all over the world." "I want to be a teacher." "I'm going to have a houseful of children." "I want to be a nurse."

Nor do life aspirations lose their grip in later years. Although many may change along the way, personal intentions retain a strong heart hold in each of us.

In those personal intentions we daily live out the first portion of Proverbs 16:9—"A man's heart deviseth his way." The second part of the verse, "but the Lord directeth his steps," may be accomplished through a physical means. Let's illustrate by going back to the girlhood life plans just mentioned.

A missionary to Bangladesh? Not if a pulmonary weakness demands avoidance of humid heat. World travel? A back injury may preclude sitting more than thirty minutes at a time. Teaching may be prevented by being stricken with deafness. The houseful of children can fail to materialize because of inability to conceive. A girl may have to forego nursing because she vomits or faints at the sight of blood.

Wherever human devising and divine direction conflict due to physical boundaries, our unrealized plans, dreams, and hopes may seem a vast empty place. If distress, anger, or depression are more than fleeting reactions, they advertise our spiritual shallowness. Yet it's difficult to keep those negatives at bay when we view dashed hopes. Why? Because our very essence dislikes boundaries of whatever sort. It prefers, always, to "do its own thing." Although salvation redeems us, it doesn't destroy the self-determining bent inherited from Eden. We continue to demonstrate that "a man's heart deviseth his way."

However spiritual our plans and dreams may seem, they are our plans. We resent anything that blocks our "devised way," and we protest the emptiness of thwarted desire.

The next three words found in Proverbs 16:9—"but the Lord"— should quiet our heart and redirect our eyes by reminding us of the Lord's oversight moment by moment. Forced departures from one's own will and way demonstrate the reality that "the Lord directeth his steps."

From our earliest years in Sunday school, we are assured that God has a perfect will for each one of us, and we are encouraged to seek it as we move forward through life. We would of course recognize God's direction if it were emblazoned in tongues of fire, written in letters of lightning across the sky, or shouted in unmistakable accents of thunder. However, our heavenly Father doesn't work that way. He often simply blocks our intended path. One such blockade may be a physical impediment.

Let's look again at the physically thwarted women presented earlier.

Pulmonary weakness, while ruling out Bangladesh, can just as clearly magnetize toward mission work among Native Americans in the desert of Arizona. The back injury that closes the door to travel may open another into junior high school instruction—where attention can best be maintained by standing while she teaches. Deafness may close out the voices of dreamed-of students yet create a passageway to Christian journalism. Inability to conceive, while it denies her biological children, can mean an opportunity to be surrogate mother to hundreds in a preschool program for underprivileged children. Physical illness at the sight of blood may well redirect this woman's attention to Christian counseling.

In each imagined instance, the emptiness seen in the physical boundary really is not that at all—it is, rather, a doorway used by the Creator to indicate His will as opposed to her will.

The principle of emptiness versus doorway is one to consider wherever and whenever we have to deal with a physical boundary. It applies to whatever limitations may be imposed by aging, as well. No place of forced decreased pace, halt, or redirection is empty in the sense of indicating God's mistake or His failure to love us. It's just the opposite—demonstration of the constant, intimate care with which He works in our lives.

For every one of us there is or will be inescapable physical restrictions that come with aging. Sometimes even in this area, our internal self frets against the external strictures. Individual chosen focus will be the deciding factor in how anyone walks the latter part of earth's pathway. Who hasn't seen the vast differences of spirit in older people? One keeps a magnifying glass trained upon aches, pains, and inabilities—and shares them with tiresome constancy. Another briefly acknowledges such things only when questioned directly and then hurries into praise for the benefits of her golden years. One pulls her mouth into lines of grumpy disapproval over youthful enjoyments around her, while another smiles at them and contributes her own laughter. One bemoans the loss of easy mobility whereas another delights in expanded opportunity to read, memorize, and meditate upon Scripture.

As we face whatever physical shortfall, keenly aware that it's crimping our personal desires, Psalm 119:15 can transform our response:

> I will meditate in thy precepts, and have respect unto thy ways.

God's precepts will clearly reveal that His way—not ours—insures His undertaking and enables us to glorify His name.

John 9 gives us a vivid illustration of God's purpose in a physical disability.

> And as Jesus passed by, he saw a man which was blind from his birth. And his disciples asked him, saying, Master, who did sin, this man, or his parents, that he was born blind? Jesus answered, Neither hath this man sinned, nor his parents: but that the works of God should be made manifest in him. (John 9:1–3)

Just as short-sighted as you and I, the disciples expressed their inability to comprehend the blind man's profound physical handicap. They analyzed the case intellectually and concluded that personal or parental sin had caused the "punishment" of blindness. Jesus swept aside those wrong diagnoses and pointed to His own purpose: demonstration of His power. The following verses tell the wonderful story of His giving the man sight.

The truth presented by Jesus' words—"that the works of God should be made manifest"—does not apply only to that man, his physical condition, and the marvel of healing. It applies to whatever physical limitation you or I may have: God desires to demonstrate His working in and through our physical structure.

Instance after instance of God's special working in, for, and through those who have physical limitations can be cited, but a few must suffice.

Fanny Crosby provides a powerful first example. Blinded as an infant by an ill-advised eye treatment, she walked in physical darkness throughout her long years of life. Yet blind eyes lent vision to her soul. In sweet submission to her heavenly Father, she not only responded with a heart song herself but also produced an enormous reservoir of songs and hymns that have richly inspired the Christian world.

But we don't need to look into the past to see admirable examples. Many of us live among those who similarly triumph over physical difficulties. Here at Bob Jones University we are blessed each year by special-case students God brings to us. Not only do they transcend varied and immense physical boundaries; their spirit also challenges and shames the rest of us. Burn victims contradict extensive physical scarring with hearts that illustrate the Lily of the Valley's beauty; the fragrance of their spirit refreshes and renews their fellow students. Those with physical disabilities requiring twenty-four-hour assistance overcome all obstacles to complete their academic degrees and also dedicate themselves to God's service on the mission field or in stateside ministries. Individuals whose bodies have been broken in automobile or industrial accidents eschew whining and complaint, instead reaching out with tender hearts to others.

Numberless real-life stories like those teach lessons of victory through submission. How great seems these folks' physical emptiness—yet how apparent is God's filling!

So the question comes to you and me: "Will I serve and glorify God in this, my body—in whatever condition He chooses?"

MENTAL LIMITATIONS

While an earlier chapter dealt with intellectual empty places, we now need to consider other "empties" of our mental structure and functioning.

Perhaps the major frustration experienced by unsaved women arises in an area of perceived competition or disadvantage: the female mind versus the male mind. Some women become irate, for instance, over a mention of contrasting brain dominance. In-arguably, God created gender differences in our mental processes: women follow a different thought path than men while moving toward similar conclusions. There's really no need for any in-depth discussion here because the matter has been addressed in earlier of my books. Suffice it to say that in the Bible God speaks His instructions to the human mind. He doesn't do a split approach between men and women except in rare instances. We born-again women ought simply to accept our mental structure as a good gift from God, intended to mesh with and complement man's, recognize both the strengths and weaknesses of our human mental apparatus, and guard our feminine mental vulnerabilities, such as over-subjectivity.

How wise the woman who makes a daily practice of submitting her mental processes to Philippians 4:8! In failing to activate this strategic mindset, we opt for emptiness after emptiness.

- Not thinking on what's true, we thrash about and bruise ourselves in the chains of empty falsehoods.
- Failing to keep our mind on that which is honest, we stumble over our own and others' empty dishonesties.

- Turning aside from just contemplations, we become bogged in the marsh of empty blame-shifting.
- Shrugging off thoughts that are pure, we ingest and infect others with empty impurities.
- Neglecting to focus upon things that are lovely, we stagger under the crushing burden of empty ugliness.
- Mentally skittering away from things that are of good report, we make ourselves and others vulnerable to empty surmising.

We each need to take God's warnings and instructions about our thoughts far more seriously than we do. Every aspect of our lives as Christians in the twenty-first century proclaims our twisted thinking. Clearly, the world rather than the Word holds sway.

DISCIPLINING OUR MIND

Scripture-obedient mental focus of course entails personal discipline; yet it's not essentially a self-induced accomplishment. The key for successfully obeying Philippians 4:8 actually lies in II Corinthians 10:5—

> Casting down imaginations, and every high thing that exalteth itself against the knowledge of God, and bringing into captivity every thought to the obedience of Christ.

The mental discipline demanded by Philippians 4:8 comes only as we conscientiously, consistently submit our mind to the mind of Christ as revealed in the Bible.

Our relationship to the Lord Jesus is the essential factor in our thought control. The better we know Him and the more intimately we walk with Him, the more we are aware of His constant examination of our internal self and the more we want that core to please Him.

Submitting our mind to the mind of Christ is done by consistently ingesting Scripture. Particularly precious to me as a basic expression of this transaction is Psalm 94:19—

> In the multitude of my thoughts within me, thy comforts delight my soul.

Those are two potent phrases. "In the multitude of my thoughts within me." Thoughts fill our mind every waking moment, amazing in their number, complexity, and variety. Computers, impressive as they are or may eventually become, pale in comparison to the human mind. There, in the "engine room" of our motivations, responses, and speech, is where God's Word can, as it were, monitor the gauges and oversee the operation.

"Thy comforts delight my soul." God speaks comforts of various sorts to the minds of His people through His Word. He comforts by giving promises, by speaking His peace, by setting forth instruction, by reminding of His love, goodness, and power. But He also comforts like an earthly parent—after rebuking and chastening us. It's then He holds us close to His heart and dries our repentant tears. God's comforting through His Word is wonderfully effective, reaching past our shallow exterior to minister His unique solace to our inmost being.

Bringing our thoughts into Christ's captivity demands a daily exchange in terms of values, perspective, and practice—all of which are constantly distorted by sin's presence in our human nature. The book of Proverbs is particularly effective in directing us toward that vital mental exchange. Solomon tells us his purpose for the collection, saying in Proverbs 1:2–4,

> To know wisdom and instruction; to perceive the words of understanding; to receive the instruction of wisdom, justice, and judgment, and equity; to give subtilty to the simple, to the young man knowledge and discretion.

That's a thorough catalog for meeting mental needs, isn't it? Why then do we order so little from the catalog? Why do we instead settle for shoddy flea-market offerings?

Rather than generalize about applying godly wisdom to our thinking, let's consider some specific instances and situations in which God-directed thoughts diverge from those that are self-directed. Psalm 17:4 is a good starting point:

> Concerning the works of men, by the word of thy lips I have kept
> me from the paths of the destroyer.

"Concerning the works of men." The works of men surround us each day, and Satan the destroyer stands ready to use them in luring us into some downward path. As the psalmist avoided that deadly intention, so may you and I if we diligently bring our thought processes into conformity to God's Word.

Many human works are positive as man uses his God-created capabilities to benefit society. Consider, for instance, marvelous scientific and medical discoveries and advances—unlocking the mysteries of DNA, performing incredible organ transplants, and inventing the x-ray, the microwave, and wireless communication. Human skill is daily evident in the design and construction of skyscrapers or delicate, handmade lace. Mortal creativity enraptures us in the art of Michelangelo, the music of Beethoven, and the literature of Shakespeare. But just as there are numberless good products of man's mind, so are there bad—the theory of evolution and financial scams. Skills are perverted into the building of horrendous car bombs and Internet pornography traps. Creativity twists art into blasphemous renderings, music into lust-provoking noise, and literature into a moral cesspool. It does not take great discernment to recognize how effectively the negative works of man are corrupting and crippling human society worldwide. We who know Christ must be able to discern between good and bad works of men—including the gray areas—and avoid being swept into the bad.

"The paths of the destroyer." We can never be over-warned about the character, the intention, and the works of our great enemy. Yet many of us brush aside Scripture warnings, choosing to believe them outdated or overstated. Modernity seeks to put a smiling face upon Apollyon, the destroyer. No doubt there is a smile—but it comes because we succumb to just such foolish self-delusion. The Devil always and only seeks to destroy. One of his pet destructive purposes is to lure God's people away from paths of righteousness via mental "baby steps." Once we set out upon any wrong path, its ultimate distance and depth can prove to be immeasurable.

Notice the word *paths*. The indicated multiplicity of Satan's descending ways is interesting. If he had only one path to destruction, we could recognize and avoid it rather easily. Instead, however, there are many routes to destruction. They are strategically placed and variously alluring. Too, they are constantly before us: Satan, a superb travel agent, advertises the charms and advantages of various itineraries whenever and wherever he senses a possible sale. And, dear reader, a mental empty place in you or me gives him just such an opportunity.

The works of men and the ploys of Satan combine to loom large indeed; an individual Christian, by contrast, is so small and weak within herself as to be overwhelmed. It's imperative that we live fully aware of the dangers and seek to be accoutered against them. Our shield of safety is the Word of God.

"By the word of thy lips I have kept me." Mental armament comes via the Bible. Its form and function appear in two verses: Proverbs 6:23 and Psalm 119:59. The first passage reads,

> For the commandment is a lamp, and the law is light; and reproofs of instruction are the way of life.

God moved Solomon to pen those words. Yes Solomon, in whom we earlier recognized a mental apparatus surpassing that of anyone else ever born. Yet here he acknowledges the natural mind's darkness, regardless of its intelligence quotient. Even the supreme human intellect could not rightly discern between available life pathways without the enlightenment of God's Word. Surely if he sought Scripture to offset mental insufficiency, so should we!

Then the psalmist weighs in:

> I thought on my ways, and turned my feet unto thy testimonies.

Here the sweet singer of Israel shares with us the crucial nature of our mortal mind in influencing our spiritual walk. God would have each of us think about our way. Doing so with a prayerful heart enables us to see both the pathway behind us with its lessons and pathways before us with their pitfalls and possibilities. Yet most believers today are walking heedlessly—paths of the past have not added learning, present pathways are empty of spiritual intent, and future routes are left to chance.

Our life on this earth is extremely brief. As God has allowed us that life in the physical sense and redeemed it in the spiritual sense, He desires that we order our walk in accordance with His mind, not our own. Choosing to do so is not a one-time decision. Initial consecration (setting out on the path of obedience) must be followed by constant pathway consideration and route choices. Every step may bring us to a crossroad, diverging routes, or an entrance or exit ramp. Without consideration and careful choice, both travel and destination can be disastrous. The necessity of consistent searching cannot be overemphasized.

At this point I want to insert a secular but thought-provoking poem by Robert Frost, "The Road Not Taken," applicable to our consideration:

Two roads diverged in a yellow wood,
And sorry I could not travel both
And be one traveler, long I stood
And looked down one as long as I could
To where it bent in the undergrowth;

Then took the other, as just as fair,
And having perhaps the better claim,
Because it was grassy and wanted wear;
Though as for that the passing there
Had worn them really about the same.

And both that morning equally lay
In leaves no step had trodden black.
Oh, I kept the first for another day!
Yet knowing how way leads on to way,
I doubted if I should ever come back.

I shall be telling this with a sigh
Somewhere ages and ages hence:
Two roads diverged in a wood, and I—
I took the one less traveled by,
And that has made all the difference.

Our pathway choices—regardless of how small they may seem—have and will, indeed, "make all the difference." I challenge you to retrace some of your own past life walk; think about the various junctures at which you made choices. Yesterday's decision to some extent shaped today's reality, didn't it?

As the psalmist thought upon his ways, realizing the import of each choice, he also recognized his mental inability to choose correctly.

Hence, he turned his feet unto God's testimonies. You and I are to do likewise. Only consistent accessing of God's infallible, inerrant Word will "make all the difference" in the positive sense spiritually.

What will that difference be, and how will it work to keep us from the paths of the destroyer?

God's testimonies—the Holy Scriptures—provide critical illumination.

> The entrance of thy words giveth light; it giveth understanding unto the simple. (Psalm 119:130)

As the spiritual skies grow darker across America and around the world, the path of right is cast into deepening shadow, increasing the danger at points of choice. Take, for instance, two matters of general lifestyle—involvements and appearance. While Scripture tells us not to forsake the old ways, it also makes clear that God is current—relevant—in all of history: The great I AM is the same yesterday, today, and forever. Nor do His people live, move, and have their being in a disconnected time warp but in the ever-living Jesus Christ. Shadows on the pathway can motivate us to choose such out-of-touch lifestyles that we lose all effectiveness of testimony. On the other hand, the shadows might cause us to so "sync" with modern life that we erase our God-demanded "set-apartness." In either case, we dishonor Christ's name and fail in our obligation to be His ambassadors. How dangerous is the darkness! How greatly we need the light of God's Word!

The Word's illumination doesn't just fall upon the pathway. It enters our very being. Because it is not of earth but of heaven, it permeates our mind, transforming our simplicity and expanding our understanding. There is enormous comfort and encouragement in knowing that we have access to God's measureless mind.

The Word of God will keep us from Satan's destructive paths by clarification.

> Through thy precepts I get understanding, therefore I hate every false way. (Psalm 119:104)

If ever there were days in which Christians need understanding in order to discern falsehood, it is these days. Satan is a master at costume and makeup. He never sends out his emissaries adorned with sandwich boards reading, BEWARE, I'M A FALSE PROPHET! Instead, he garbs them in respectable, attractive outfits; tones, texture, and labels project an image of rightness. How carefully our foe attends to the deceivers' faces: softly gleaming eyes and gentle smiles enhance smooth words; rationale is subtle and strong; assurances are sweetened by frequent Bible quotations.

A mind in tune only to earth is easily deceived, but a mind drawing upon heavenly resources sees what lies behind the disguises— poison in the palaver. As a result of that God-given clarification, the believer not only avoids the false way; she hates it.

The lack of "holy hatred" so characterizing modern Christianity is one of our greatest weaknesses. Rather than detesting the false ways around us, we look upon them casually, or even with yearning. We've accepted the constantly expounded theme of "tolerance," convinced that anything else shows a lack of love. Genuine love, however, hates that which besmirches its beloved. The kind of anything-goes tolerance painted so boldly on modernity's banner has nothing to do with eternity's credo.

Ye that love the Lord, hate evil. (Psalm 97:10)

Weak hatred of evil indicates weak love for God. Intake of God's Word is absolutely essential in accurately identifying evil and rightly responding to it. It's important to remember that God-loving hatred for evil is not a foaming-at-the-mouth, ugly-spirited, saber-tongued, obnoxious, monstrous persona. Proper hatred of evil looks, acts, and speaks like Jesus Christ.

The words of God keep us from the destroyer's paths by direction.

Thy testimonies also are my delight and my counselors. (Psalm 119:24)

In considering the importance of Bible intake, we might mistakenly conclude that study of and immersion in it must be a determined, stringently enforced, nobly endured undertaking. Wrong. Intake of the precious, all-essential Word of God should be a unique, unexcelled delight as we experience a magnetic beckoning from God's heart to ours.

In conclusion, each of us should accept her mental structure as God's loving, wise creation and submit it to His constant scrutiny and instruction.

Search me, O God, and know my heart: try me, and know my thoughts: and see if there be any wicked way in me, and lead me in the way everlasting. (Psalm 139:23–24)

Emotional Limitations

Only a few considerations are necessary as we look at our emotional processes due to extensive coverage in *The Wilderness Within*.

First, it is important to stress the positives of God's emotional design in us women: our emotional capacity is a good part of our structure. This blessed gift, however, is always under attack by our archenemy. One of his most effective tactics is double-pronged: to tighten our emotional focus while loosening our emotional control.

Second, emotional involvement per se is an aspect of our unified composition—body, mind, and spirit (or soul); they do not operate separately but are intertwined. However, our emotions tend to be magnifiers, and they most consistently magnify negatives—whether in experience, in people, or in ourselves. Negative magnification in turn produces or worsens negative responses and results. Women who speak to me about wide-ranging kinds of emptiness demonstrate that their emotions are embroiled, exacerbating the core problem.

Third, emotions defy human control. Being a person strongly given to visualizing concepts, I picture my emotional self as a teardrop-shaped vessel. It's a valuable vessel, and the contents are precious when rightly dispensed. At the same time, however, the container is slippery, defying the grasp of my hands. Its base is rounded, making it incapable of stability. As the acid of wrong thinking drips or pours down into the vessel, the contents stir, foam, and rise, tipping the container and spewing the roiled contents in all directions. How, then, does one successfully deal with such a vessel and bring it under control? By putting handles on it. Then and only then does it become manageable. One handle is the Word of God in my mind; the other handle is the Holy Spirit's active operation in my soul. I must enlist both handles for successful emotional control.

The words *emotional* and *female* are sometimes spoken jointly and with negative overtones. While we dislike the inference, it's easy to see how it becomes a common complaint against us: wrong expressions of emotion cause trouble and pain. I'd urge you to look seriously at the many passages in Proverbs that deal with emotionally negative women; words such as *brawling* and *contentious* describe them. Then move on to Ecclesiastes, where Solomon says,

> And I find more bitter than death the woman, whose heart is snares and nets, and her hands are bands (Ecclesiastes 7:26).

The feminine heart described there is one of intense self-focus and self-seeking: a misuse of emotions. When self reigns in our emotions, it creates the emptiness of grasping, discontent, and misery.

By contrast, the psalmist experienced the source of emotional fullness.

> My meditation of him shall be sweet; I will be glad in the Lord. (Psalm 104:34)

Sweetness and gladness characterize an emotional state far different from those mentioned earlier.

The New Testament also contains many passages that encourage proper and positive emotions. For instance, there is the apostle Paul's benedictory urging.

> Now the God of hope fill you with all joy and peace in believing, that ye may abound in hope, through the power of the Holy Ghost. (Romans 15:13)

Joy and peace—what a marvelous picture of emotional fullness. But how many of us Christian women consistently present that picture? I know a few such women—a very few. Being in their company at any time is a blessing. In those dear, rare ladies there's rich overflow from their vessels of emotion.

Miserable, self-propelled emotionalism is rebuked when we look at the God we're called to emulate and reflect. His great heart is seen repeatedly—and it reminds us how far short we fall as reflectors of His heart.

> But thou, O Lord, art a God full of compassion, and gracious, longsuffering, and plenteous in mercy and truth. (Psalm 86:15)

> The Lord is gracious, and full of compassion; slow to anger, and of great mercy. (Psalm 145:8)

Note in both passages the words and phrases indicating emotion-related divine characteristics:

- Compassion
- Gracious
- Longsuffering
- Plenteous in mercy and truth
- Slow to anger
- Of great mercy

They are outflow from God's heart—each one powerful in itself and beneficial in its effects. How unlike the typical emotional manifestations of the human heart! The dissimilarity strikes me with conviction even as I write the words. Our hearts seek our own filling, whereas God's heart seeks others' filling.

It would be wonderful if our contemplation of the divine heart would move us to alter our own. Such alteration demands that we first siphon off the acid of wrong thinking and the selfishness that hoards emotion's spikenard for our own gratification. Then by His empowering we can grasp the handles of our heart's alabaster jar and let the fragrant balm of His heart-work in us flow forth for others. In so doing we will learn it's in emptying ourselves that we are filled. We would then be replete with the quieting assurance of Isaiah 58:11—

> And the Lord shall guide thee continually, and satisfy thy soul in drought, and make fat thy bones: and thou shalt be like a watered garden, and like a spring of water, whose waters fail not.

The acid-foamed, unbalanced vessel of emotions always whines, "I need!" The Word-and-Spirit-handled vessel instead whispers, "What do you need?"

THINKING IT OVER

The older I get and the more I'm in the Scripture, the clearer it becomes that these mortal bodies in which we live have a ball-and-chain effect upon our immortal spirit. Though our heart yearns toward our Savior, every step we take is slowed and hindered by the dragging weight, the bruising shackles, and the clanking chains of our flesh.

The poetess Christina Rossetti beautifully captured our flesh-versus-spirit trouble. Let your heart ponder the final lines.

> God, harden me against myself,
> This coward with pathetic voice
> Who craves for ease, and rest, and joys:

Myself, arch-traitor to myself;
My hollowest friend, my deadliest foe,
My clog whatever road I go.
Yet One there is can curb myself,
Can roll the strangling load from me,
Break off the yoke and set me free.

CHAPTER SIX

EMPTINESS IN PREPARATION

THERE IS A GENERATION THAT CURSETH THEIR FATHER, AND
DOTH NOT BLESS THEIR MOTHER.

PROVERBS 30:11

Some women sense emptiness because of areas in which they feel
inadequately equipped for successful living. There are several mentioned repeatedly by counselees.

HOME BACKGROUND SHORTFALL

Each of us is a composite of varied and numerous influences. The
most profound of those is the home in which we grew up. Adulthood finds many women struggling over shortfall in their childhood home's provision. Let's examine some typical empty places
blamed upon faulty home background.

Character. "Sharon" recognizes poor character qualities in herself—dishonesty, blame-shifting, lack of integrity, laziness, lack of
tenacity, and so forth. She looks back upon her youth and realizes
that she was never challenged to develop her character. Her parents

tolerated her unlovely spirit and actions and excused her faults. Now her character weaknesses create daily problems in her personal relationships and her professional attainment. In the face of mature life challenges, she rues the winds of emptiness emanating from what she lacked at home.

Social ability. "Mary Ellen" feels awkward in meeting people, has difficulty carrying on conversations, and fears situations that demand knowledge of etiquette. She regretfully reflects upon her home's insufficient social preparation. No emphasis was put upon even the most basic principles of meeting people, social behavior, or table manners. Real conversation hardly existed outside of shouted commands or disinterested grunts. Married to a professional man, she agonizes over the constant social demands upon them as a couple. Her every backward glance locates emptiness. The winds from yesterday chill her today.

Confidence. Having expected adulthood to bring a flowering of positive attitude and courage to face challenges, "Teresa" may experience tremendous disappointment when she instead continues to battle self-doubt, shrinking in the face of challenges. Looking back to the home where she grew up, she replays her older sister's taunts, her mother's unfavorable comparisons of her with her sister, and her father's scornful comments about her frequent failures. Keenly aware of how empty she is of confidence, she rues the draining effect of her home, and the wind sighs mournfully of her resultant need.

Negativism. When friends point out her pervasive tendency to gloominess, "Belinda" is merely confirmed in the lifelong gray skies of her attitude. Searching for reasons, she reviews her younger years, through which her mother existed in a state of grim, complaining determination while her father tried to drown his depression in alcohol. Belinda yearns for release from the cave of her empty, echoing yesterdays.

The examples given are only a few home-rooted lacks commonly experienced. Sad to contemplate in others, they're even sadder to recognize in ourselves. The profound influence of our childhood home's formative power may seem to create inescapable emptiness. But does it?

Our flesh wants to use deficiencies like those mentioned as platforms from which to frown back helplessly upon an imperfect childhood home. Instead, the Christian woman can deny the flesh and activate faith. She will then recognize any background-generated void as an open place in which God can work with wonderful intimacy and power. As the psalmist said,

> When my father and my mother forsake me, then the Lord will take me up (Psalm 27:10).

Parental "forsaking" occurs in many different ways, and the term would apply to inadequate parenting like the types just mentioned. The promised divine compensation applies to all cases— and we must put away our sense of entrapment and reach up to take His lifting hand. Many of us can joyfully testify of His faithful, loving response. As He takes us up, the Lord also moves forward with us step by step to fullness in the areas of our need. Rethink how that might play out in the cases mentioned earlier.

Character. Are you like "Sharon?" Acknowledging home-rooted character weakness is good; blaming the root and nurturing its weedy outgrowth is not. Take a moment to personalize the challenge Paul the apostle originally presented to Timothy in II Timothy 2:1—

> Thou therefore, my son, be strong in the grace that is in Christ Jesus.

Those words present the blessed essential for all genuine spiritual strength: Christ's enabling grace. With that concept firmly in mind we can move forward with our private internal strength-building project.

At each point you perceive personal weakness, go to the book of Proverbs. Think carefully as you read. What comes through in the attitudes, speech, and actions depicted? Clearly, it's present choice—not past chains. That being the case, weak character can be strengthened bit by bit, one point of failure at a time. Just as flabby muscles gain strength through exercise, so does flabby character. God is Himself strong, and He wants His children to be strong.

First Timothy 4:7 puts it this way:

> Exercise thyself rather unto godliness.

Every day of life presents numberless opportunities for such exercise. At point after point we have to forsake the sofa of self-coddling and get busy with character aerobics. In other words, we should ask the Lord's help for His essential strengthening within our core, then do the hard thing. Ultimately we'll be able to say with the psalmist,

> In the day when I cried thou answeredst me, and strengthenedst
> me with strength in my soul (Psalm 138:3).

As soul strength grows, outward evidences will multiply.

While determination to strengthen character is basic, upon that foundation we must lay bricks of daily, practical diligence. Help for such important effort is found throughout the Bible. Our blessed Operator's Manual is packed with condemnation of weak character qualities and encouragement for strong ones. And, of course, the source of our strengthening is clearly presented over and over again throughout the Word.

> The Lord is my rock, and my fortress, and my deliverer; my
> God, my strength, in whom I will trust; my buckler, and the
> horn of my salvation, and my high tower. (Psalm 18:2)

> Finally, my brethren, be strong in the Lord, and in the power of
> his might. (Ephesians 6:10)

Recognizing God's desire for our strength, His ability to help us toward it, and His provision of it in Himself, we can move forward to overcome our character failings—regardless of our home's failure.

Social unease. If, like "Mary Ellen," you experience difficulties socially, cut off the useless cord of blame that ties you to missed instruction. Bind yourself, instead, to spiritual and practical retraining. Misery in social situations mainly rises from a wrong focus: concentration on yourself—how you feel, what impression you may be making, what you can say and how you can say it to impress or be well-received, and so forth. Self-focus guarantees discomfort unless you're a supreme egotist! God would have us turn our focus away from ourselves and onto others.

> Look not every man on his own things, but every man also on
> the things of others. (Philippians 2:4)

That principle is not applicable only in the general, overall sense; it should also come into play each day in relational and social matters.

The change of focus, however, should not just be a force of will. Rather, proper refocusing demands whole-self involvement so that the motivation is not our own comfort and confidence but genuine love for others.

First John 4:9–10 reminds us how God's saving love was manifested to us: He sent His Son, Jesus Christ, to pay the penalty for our sins. Then verse 11 tells us how we should respond to that divine love:

> Beloved, if God so loved us, we ought also to love one another.

If you and I genuinely develop a loving focus on others, our social self will not only experience loosening from tension and timidity but will also present a magnetic testimony for the Lord. Conversational difficulties will ease when we operate on the fuel of genuine interest in the person to whom we're talking.

Brotherly love should also motivate us to become proficient in matters of etiquette. Why? Because proper manners say "I care enough about other people to behave correctly." Poor manners are offensive to those around us; more importantly, they blacken the name of the Lord.

Manners are merely habits of behavior; therefore, they can be improved. Etiquette is one means of polishing our all-too-earthen selves in order to reflect Jesus Christ. There is no need or excuse for a Christian woman to remain socially inept due to her home background. She simply needs to care enough about others and her own testimony to work toward good habits of etiquette. For further consideration, *In the Best Possible Light* deals with the subject of etiquette in depth and detail.

Confidence. Those of us who, like "Teresa," are not naturally outgoing look upon self-confident folks around us with admiration, wishing that we could move through life in similar ease. When the wind of emptiness blows over us from the icy pond of insecurity, we mustn't let it freeze us into immobility or send us into flight. Listen to the wind; identify its true message. Insecurity is a type of fear: fear of exposure, failure, or embarrassment or fear of others' scrutiny, dislike, or opposition.

The goal for a Christian woman seeking to overcome crippling insecurity should not be increased self-assurance but exchange of her emptiness for the fullness of Jesus Christ.

> My flesh and my heart faileth; but God is the strength of my heart, and my portion for ever. (Psalm 73:26)

It is better to trust in the Lord than to put confidence in man. (Psalm 118:8)

In the truest sense, self-confidence in a born-again Christian is not a positive, but a negative: it stems from pride. Instead, we need to relinquish our fearful insecurity and tighten our heart hold upon the Savior.

In the fear of the Lord is strong confidence: and his children shall have a place of refuge. (Proverbs 14:26)

The Lord shall be thy confidence, and shall keep thy foot from being taken. (Proverbs 3:26)

For thus saith the high and lofty One that inhabiteth eternity, whose name is Holy: I dwell in the high and holy place, with him also that is of a contrite and humble spirit, to revive the spirit of the humble and to revive the heart of the contrite ones. (Isaiah 57:15)

Negativism. When this attitude discoloration—as exemplified in "Belinda"—begins in childhood, the deepness of the dye may seem permanent. John Milton wrote in *Paradise Lost*,

> The mind is its own place, and in itself
> Can make a heav'n of hell, a hell of heav'n.

Gloom and hopelessness, however, are antithetical to the God Who is light and hope. When our spiritual position moves closer and closer to Jesus Christ, our attitudinal disposition will brighten, as well. Just as He saves from sin, so too He wants to save from negativism's echoing cavern.

I am the Lord thy God, which brought thee out of the land of Egypt: open thy mouth wide, and I will fill it. (Psalm 81:10)

That verse powerfully connects God's ability to save our soul with His continuing ability to supply our empty places.

The news media so constantly bombards us with graphic reminders of terrorist attacks, natural disasters, threatened financial collapse, murder, and mayhem, it's no wonder when unsaved people move through their days with a negative mindset and a hopeless spirit. Their various self-empowered "positives" are pathetic, frail things. But we who know Christ can lay hold of eternal verities and thereby live in unshakable hope.

> Our help is in the name of the Lord, who made heaven and earth. (Psalm 124:8)

A woman struggling against deeply ingrained negativism will protest, "But I don't feel positive!" She's stating the truth. Negativism flows from inward heaviness—a weight that denies there is hope and help from our Burden Bearer. Scripture pictures such a person and presents a hand-up.

> Heaviness in the heart of man maketh it stoop; but a good word maketh it glad. (Proverbs 12:25)

"A good word" can apply, of course, to that which comes from human lips, and the stated principle can motivate us to encourage folks around us. But in a far greater way the passage points us to the ultimate good word—the Bible—and its weight-relieving effect. It's imperative for a woman who tends toward negativism to counteract that tendency with daily intake of Scripture.

A positive outlook on life doesn't depend upon the past, the present, or the future—no matter what they may hold. Rather, it comes as we anchor our soul with the mighty chain of Scripture.

> Let all those that seek thee rejoice and be glad in thee: and let such as love thy salvation say continually, Let God be magnified. (Psalm 70:4)

A Christian whose spirit exudes negativism (even—or especially—if she claims it to be "spiritual") contradicts the message of the

Bible and the newness of life in Jesus Christ. A negative spirit is light years removed from that expressed in Psalm 119:162:

> I rejoice at thy word, as one that findeth great spoil.

The Word reveals the Christian's source of positive spirit as much more than just a cross-my-fingers, figure-it-will-turn-out-okay type. Rather, ours is a vital, vibrant, interpersonal transaction with the King of Kings.

> For thou art my hope, O Lord God; thou art my trust from my youth. (Psalm 71:5)

Gloom may have surrounded you in your childhood home—but why do you let it cling? The "glue" of its attachment to your spirit may seem permanent; however, its bonding is your own choice. Draw near to the heart of your heavenly Father, and the warmth of His great heart will melt the glue that binds you to the past.

EDUCATIONAL DEFICIENCY

Sometimes in listening to a woman talk, I'm amazed how quickly she will point to her educational history as her perceived emptiness:

- "I didn't finish high school."
- "I started college but dropped out due to finances."
- "We got married right after high school."
- "No one ever made me study or challenged me to be serious in my schooling."
- "The only school in our area was a small country type shunned by good teachers."
- "I attended an inner city school where the teachers just put in their hours and tried not to antagonize the rough kids."
- "There was no Christian school available in our section of the country."

— "We tried homeschooling for a while, but my parents gave up and sent me back to public school."

A woman may allow such feelings of educational emptiness to be a dragging burden or a daunting barrier. If so, she is letting Satan befoul her "empty place."

God is not restricted to scholastic accomplishment or academic degrees. My heart hurts when a woman refers to her educational lacks with embarrassment or in protest against her ability to do what God has called her to do. I learned while young that wisdom and education are totally different things. In thinking through my own extended family, I can point to various ones who highlighted that fact. My mother finished only two years of high school. But in every area of her life she displayed an active intellect, solid common sense, and gentle spiritual wisdom—with all of it wrapped in a happy little package of warm practicality. By contrast, there were some on both sides of the family who not only completed high school but also went on through college and then earned advanced degrees. Their technical knowledge did little to enhance either their daily life or their character. In fact, in some instances the reverse was true: pride in or dependence upon their formal training narrowed their accomplishment and diminished their being.

A Christian woman considering her formal education and scholastic capabilities must silence the yammering inner voice that tells her they're inadequate. Then, in quietness, she needs to wait before the Lord for His perspective.

> Wait on the Lord, and keep his way, and he shall exalt thee to inherit the land. (Psalm 37:34)

If our desire is to "keep his way," we can have confidence that He has chosen and prepared us for that way. His choice for each one of us was made before He founded the earth; His creation of us was a considered, unique knitting together of parts in our mother's womb. His preparation of us has taken place through all of our past according to His perfect knowledge of our present and our future. Knowing the end from the beginning, He works for the purpose of His glory throughout our entire life span. Applying that wondrous truth to our educational preparation, each of us can be assured that

- He gave me adequate mental capacity.
- He gave me adequate mental capability.
- He gave me adequate training opportunity.

What if your quiet waiting before the Lord reveals to you that you failed to honor the opportunity of training He gave—opting out, dropping out, or lazing through somewhere along the educational trail? Then you should

- Confess the past failure.
- Determine to use your mind well now to the fullest of your ability.
- Take advantage of whatever current study opportunity may open to you.

Be assured of God's forgiveness and compensation. Compensational learning is most obviously and powerfully available in the eternal Textbook.

> Then shall I not be ashamed, when I have respect unto all thy commandments. (Psalm 119:6)

The meaning of *respect* in that verse means to "look into."

Study of our essential Text will clarify the contrast between the "smarts" emanating from man and the encompassing wisdom of God.

> The instruction of fools is folly. (Proverbs 16:22)

> Wisdom is the principal thing; therefore get wisdom: and with
> all thy getting get understanding. (Proverbs 4:7)

The wisdom extolled throughout the book of Proverbs is not earthly intelligence but godly mental and spiritual endowment. Its every characteristic originated in God and was displayed by the person of Jesus Christ. Hear, then, what the Lord—eternal Wisdom—would say to any of us bemoaning educational empty places.

> All the words of my mouth are in righteousness; there is nothing
> froward or perverse in them. They are all plain to him that
> understandeth, and right to them that find knowledge. (Proverbs
> 8:8–9)

> Counsel is mine, and sound wisdom: I am understanding; I have
> strength. (Proverbs 8:14)

> I love them that love me; and those that seek me early shall find
> me. (Proverbs 8:17)

Spiritual Unpreparedness

Those who yearn to be all they can be for the Lord may have an ache of longing for the kind of background that would have provided spiritual benefit to their present life. The empty place seems to guarantee insufficiency. Following are a few emptiness expressions made to me by women in far-flung places and of diverse life stages, professions, and personalities.

- "I grew up in an unsaved family."
- "All I knew in childhood was the fluffy teaching of a liberal church."
- "My parents took us children from one cult to another."
- "I really didn't even read the Bible until I was eighteen."

＊   "My father and mother were members of a witches'
coven. They regularly used Bible passages in their blasphemous rites."

Reading through that list certainly produces sympathy for a
child so reared. But just as in the other areas discussed, so in this:
the vacancy of the past, rather than legislating present weakness or
failure, can instead encourage intensified spiritual desire, growth,
and service. Two examples from Scripture of individuals whose
backgrounds contradict spiritual preparedness come immediately
to mind: Rahab and the apostle Paul.

All of us who are familiar with the Bible and its characters automatically link Rahab's name with her profession in Jericho: "Rahab
the harlot." Surely that designation indicates a profoundly inadequate spiritual heritage! But at a critical moment Rahab turned her
back on all she had ever known. She protected Israel's spies and
thereby escaped Jericho's devastation. She was also transported to
an entirely new life. In experience, in culture, and in matters of faith
she certainly could have pointed to empty places, couldn't she? But
her acceptance of and adoption into the faith of her former enemies
was so thorough that God looked upon her with special favor. In
His marvelous grace, He not only adopted her into His spiritual
family but also granted her a place in the human genealogy of His
Son, Jesus Christ!

As for Saul of Tarsus, he espoused the extreme opposite of
Christian belief and was determined to exterminate those who
named the name of Christ. His years of formal training and study
were in well-known Jewish schools. But then God accosted Saul
on the road to Damascus. In that instant everything changed. Although his body continued along his intended route, his heart and
soul reversed direction. Hatred for Christ became fervent love;
fury against believers became sacrificial ministry to them. Saul-

become-Paul didn't complain about wasted years or lack of appropriate training—he simply moved forward with faith in and service for his Savior.

Effective Christian life ministry doesn't result from earthly sources of spiritual nurture or instruction, but from heaven's teaching through personal enrollment in the Bible's unique curriculum. The education toward which God urges each one of us is that of personal spiritual growth: mind and heart unified in ever-increasing focus upon and obedience to His eternally settled Text.

In his first letter to Timothy, a young pastor in Ephesus, Paul wrote a potent prescription for spiritual effectiveness.

> Meditate upon these things; give thyself wholly to them, that thy profiting may appear to all. (I Timothy 4:15)

The elements in that prescription can contribute to our own spiritual health.

"Meditate upon these things." God wants us to get into the depths of His Word, not just skitter over the surface like water bugs. The Bible is immeasurably deep, and as we move from shallow to deep we will constantly discover expanded meaning, relevance, and power.

"Give thyself wholly to them." Real immersion in Scripture involves concentration, acceptance, response, and application. God doesn't direct His Word to technical scholars; He communicates through it to personal learners.

"That thy profiting may appear to all." Here's the essential, individualized aspect reiterated. We are to seek from Scripture personal instruction and enrichment. When that genuinely takes place, the results will be apparent to and profitable for onlookers—not as a matter of effective outlines or eloquent words but of Christ filling our lives.

THINKING IT OVER

In each of the areas discussed in this chapter, the purported empty places have to do with earthly supply and preparation. Our flesh yearns for that which human sources are thought to provide. It's our manner of thinking that really is the empty place. Hear, then, and take to heart the Holy Spirit's urging from Ephesians 4.

> This I say, therefore, and testify in the Lord, that ye henceforth walk not as other Gentiles walk, in the vanity of their mind, having the understanding darkened, being alienated from the life of God through the ignorance that is in them, because of the blindness of their heart: who being past feeling have given themselves over to lasciviousness, to work all uncleanness with greediness. But ye have not so learned Christ; if so be that ye have heard him, and have been taught by him, as the truth is in Jesus: that ye put off concerning the former conversation the old man, which is corrupt according to the deceitful lusts; and be renewed in the spirit of your mind, and that ye put on the new man, which after God is created in righteousness and true holiness. (Ephesians 4:17–24)

CHAPTER SEVEN

EXPERIENTIAL EMPTINESS

THEN I LOOKED ON ALL THE WORKS THAT MY HANDS HAD
WROUGHT, AND ON THE LABOUR THAT I HAD LABOURED TO
DO; AND BEHOLD, ALL WAS VANITY AND VEXATION OF SPIRIT,
AND THERE WAS NO PROFIT UNDER THE SUN.

ECCLESIASTES 2:11

The taste buds of our human essence are set for sweets and cream;
life, however, serves up a more extensive menu including sour, salty,
bitter, and gritty. Just as our bodies depend greatly upon water and
consistently thirst for it, so our inner being yearns for invigorating
experiential streams. But life more often presents mud puddles or
swamps. Somewhere along the way comes disappointment: what
we hoped for fails to become reality. Wherever the specific point of
unfulfilled expectations lies, we may hear the sighing wind of emptiness. Let's examine three areas of experience in which we women
may hunger and thirst: significance, success, and satisfaction.

SIGNIFICANCE

One of the things that strike me forcibly as I travel and entertain
myself with people-watching is their obvious, constant striving to

prove personal significance. Business and professional folks do so openly and brashly, touting their assignments, degrees, training, accomplishments, schedules, positions, connections, awards, and so forth. But private individuals, as well, fill their conversations with self-puffing descriptions, revelations, and explanations. That tendency is not confined to the traveling public. It's in the warp and woof of humanity's fabric. Christians generally seek to sublimate its expression, recognizing pride's part in such obvious bids for recognition. But whether sublimated or openly expressed, the yearning for significance is a normal thread in our structure.

The world at large decrees that people who "matter" have lives marked with interesting, fulfilling experiences—an existence that throbs with goings, comings, and doings. The contrast between such glitzy involvements and our own quiet tenor of life can—occasionally or consistently—awaken a sighing wind of emptiness.

What is personal significance, anyway? It's a sense of having meaning in and of oneself—of mattering somehow in the overall scheme of things. Yet daily life, with its fleeting hours, its mindless tasks, its generally unexceptional flow, can make us women feel wholly expendable. Our tiny personal contribution to life may seem unnecessary or even wasted: "Anyone at all could take my place, and I'd never be missed. I just don't matter!"

How do we come to such a state of mind? A number of pathways may take us to that lonely spot marked "Insignificance," but the ones we seem to travel most often are comparison and commendation.

All of us know women who are movers and shakers: they're prominent in the community, their profession, or the political world. They go places; they do things. As you and I sit at home in a housecoat reading about them in the morning newspaper, we seem far removed from such significance. Thus, comparison assigns us to mediocrity or failure.

Of course we know—in our head—that comparisons are odious. Our mind acknowledges the truth of II Corinthians 10:12:

> But they measuring themselves by themselves, and comparing themselves among themselves, are not wise.

Nevertheless, we use unequal weights on the comparison scales, according to our predetermined purpose. We overload someone—or anyone—else's scale dish in order to prove that we're the lightweight in significance. The Bible rebukes us in Proverbs 20:23.

> Divers weights are an abomination unto the Lord, and a false balance is not good.

Verbalized approval is sweet encouragement to any soul, and it makes us feel significant. But how often do we ordinary women receive such heartening input? The general answer is rarely, and in some cases, sadly, it's never. There are two major reasons women come up short in verbalized approval: our own position and others' personal focus.

A woman's life is generally not in the spotlight. A married woman's main world is home and family; a single woman, even though in a public profession, most often serves in a supporting role. Life's spotlights focus elsewhere; spotlighted roles naturally receive applause, while those outside the spotlight are pretty much unnoticed.

As for others' personal focus, it's daily evident that people around us are wrapped up in their own concerns and thus unaware of or uninterested in our performance, interests, and needs. When people fail to recognize, value, and commend us, we're not only disappointed and perhaps discouraged but also tempted to resent their self-absorption.

When troubled by a wind moaning this emptiness, we need to step back and refocus. "I just don't matter!" can be accurately translated "Poor me," can't it? That's self-pity, pure and simple. Yet we descend into self-pity time after time. And the slide can continue down into any number of ugly negative depths.

Let's take a vision-clearing step back. Just why, how, and to whom do we want to be significant? Brutal honesty uncovers some unflattering answers.

Why? Because if I felt more important, I'd feel better about myself.

How? Someone needs to notice me (more). People around me should say that I'm important to them.

To whom? Whoever has—in my estimation—failed to recognize and applaud my being or my doings.

Read through those again. Doesn't something pop out at you? It should! S-e-l-f is there in all its glory—see it in "I" ... "I'm" ... "I'd" ... "myself" ... "me" ... "my" ... "my being" ... "my doings" ... Whew!

Let's crawl out of the pit to stand on the level ground of actuality. Each one of us as a born-again believer has significance. Whatever our feeling to the contrary, the fact is revealed in the Bible's pages. No matter how many times you may have read them, go back now and really absorb them:

- God designed and created each one of us: Psalm 139:14–16.
- Jesus Christ paid the ultimate price for our salvation: I Peter 1:18–19.
- Our heavenly Father constantly watches over us: Psalm 139:17–18.

Therefore, when wind begins to flutter our frailty with "I just don't matter!" let's replace the drooping pennant of self-pity with the bold banner of Scripture. Jeremiah 9:23–24 effectively sets aside human significance measurements, replacing them with the one genuine indicator of our individual meaning:

Thus saith the Lord, Let not the wise man glory in his wisdom, neither let the mighty man glory in his might, let not the rich man glory in his riches: but let him that glorieth glory in this,

that he understandeth and knoweth me, that I am the Lord
which exercise lovingkindness, judgment, and righteousness, in
the earth: for in these things I delight, saith the Lord.

Pity turned inward is debilitating but if properly directed—
outward—can motivate great good. God so pitied you and me as
we were held in the death-grip of sin that He sacrificed His Son
Jesus Christ to release us. When we pity someone else's need, we
can reach out to encourage and help them; therein we demonstrate
significance as a conduit of God's wondrous love.

SUCCESS

The modern world constantly and strongly appeals to humanity's
front-runner bent, and we Christians can absorb worldly evaluations of success despite our intentions to resist them. Billboards,
newspapers, magazines, television, and radio bombard us with attainment messages: "Anyone who really attains has a life marked by
one or more of the following."

- Energetic good health (with no bunions, wrinkles, or
  constipation)
- A dream house
- A scintillating social life
- A closet full of the latest fashions
- Mind-stimulating activities
- Vacations in exotic places
- Recognition in a worthwhile (publicly acclaimed) profession
- An income enabling ease and luxury

In reading that list, we would ordinarily mock it as ridiculous,
but when the list as a whole or in part takes on reality by contrast to
our own existence, the false measurements can challenge the ones

we know to be accurate. Consider how it might be so in each of the categories listed above.

Energetic good health? It may elude us from birth, be snatched from us by disease or accident, and will surely leave us in old age. Whatever the timing, the means, or the extent of hampered health, grinning promoters of vitamins and over-muscled gurus of exercise mock us. When health issues prevent our experiencing the maximum in activities, attitudes, and accomplishments, we may struggle with a sense of emptiness.

A dream house? That doesn't necessarily translate to mansion. Your ideal, instead, may be a log cabin on a lake or a simple one-story on a horse ranch or a city condo or a suburban split-level. Whatever its yearned-for specifications, that imagined ideal abode may never materialize. Instead of the log cabin on the lake, you live in a bustling, smog-filled city. Your third-floor apartment is a far cry from the horse ranch single-story. Though you yearn for a modern city condo, you're ensconced in a small-town Victorian monstrosity. That multi-level suburban place has never come to be; your domicile has wheels under it—an evangelist's travel unit. However the dream picture has been redrawn, there's the possibility of emptiness in the substitute reality.

A scintillating social life? As a lifetime single you spend your days at the office and your evenings reading, crafting, watching TV, or having a rare dinner out with friends. Or as the mother of young children, socializing is limited to passing comments between you and your fellow carpoolers. The wished-for, missing sparkle can be painful.

A closet full of the latest fashions? Even as a child, you may have had a penchant for clothes. And your sense of style is a gift inherited from your mother. Dress departments and boutiques draw you magnetically. Throughout your teens you anticipated an adulthood that would make possible a "just right" wardrobe. Instead, your life path has brought you to a logging camp where only denim, flannel, and coarse wool are sensible. In terms of expectations, your closet is empty.

Mind-stimulating activities? Siblings and friends often complained that you didn't want to join them for imaginative games or for sports. Instead, your interest was in reading. You took in every word in the daily newspaper, read encyclopedia entries for fun, and studied a wide variety of subjects just for the challenge of new learning. Although your aspirations were never voiced, they centered upon professions demanding intellectual challenge. Yet here you are, bound round-the-clock to managing a restaurant that your husband inherited from his parents shortly after you were married. Because he also inherited poor health, you necessarily shoulder the load as breadwinner. When you wipe the tables clean at night, you look down into the reflected face of disappointed hopes.

Vacations in exotic places? "Faraway shores" has been a haunting mental refrain for as long as you can remember. You bought travel magazines with your very first baby-sitting paycheck when you were twelve years old. Cutout illustrations of famous sites around the world plastered your bedroom walls through high school and college, and you amassed an impressive collection of brochures from cruise lines and travel organizations. But you have a workaholic husband who looks upon vacations only as interruptions that he must avoid. In those rare instances when he can be pulled away from the office, he grumblingly loads you and the family up for an overnight camping trip at a spot five miles out of town. Cooking over the open fire, your eyes fill with tears as you see in the rising smoke your forever-faraway places.

Recognition in a worthwhile profession? High school and college teachers excitedly encouraged your gifts. Obviously a people person, you're also adept at organization, financial matters, and administration. As you enjoyed easy success throughout your school years, your mind moved ahead to a career in the business world. Yet here you are now—a mother of five children produced in seven years, with another one on the way. Life seems to have shrunk to the tiny circumference of laundry room, kitchen, and nursery. Amid the screams of your squabbling children, you hear the echo of emptiness.

An income enabling ease and luxury? You grew up in a home where financial existence was pretty much hand-to-mouth. You not only had to earn your own way but also had to contribute to your family's needs. You saw your friends spend their youth free from the need to work, enjoying the benefits of overly generous allowances and unconcerned about the price on whatever they wanted. Despite the difficulties, you stayed cheerful and optimistic as you focused on a future worthy of the term "golden." But that future has became a rerun of the past: your father died before you finished high school, and your sickly mother became your responsibility. Her constantly worsening condition continues to drain away everything you earn. At the end of an exhausting day both outside and inside the house, you cry yourself to sleep in the emptiness of shattered dreams and aching body.

However experience fails to match our heart-sketched success site, we may be tempted to scrawl "Empty!" across the substituted life canvas. But let's pause a moment to look again at the substitution that—at least momentarily—has us thinking it is a cruel forgery.

The trouble actually began many years ago when we allowed the artist Imaginative Expectations to take up the paintbrush. She—oh yes, she's a woman—dipped the brush into the brightest, boldest colors on her palette and applied them to the canvas, creating an idyllic landscape. The painting she produced was so lovely that we felt immediate affection for it. Then we hung the picture in a prime viewing spot.

Only trouble results when we engage I. Expectations. She is highly skilled, taking top honors in the school of illusion. She doesn't attempt to paint realistically, but her works are highly pleasant. So we stand tearful or angry because the lovely painting is a lie.

Now let's dry our tears, put away anger, and turn our critical—not craving—gaze upon Expectations' work. The colors she used aren't really bright, but gaudy. The forms she chose to fill the canvas are actually not reasonable, as we'd thought, but surreal. Those are the characteristics of illusion's school of painting.

The fault, dear reader, is our own. We employed the wrong artist and accepted her lying representation. We need to replace the illusionary picture with the priceless masterpiece God intends.

It was I. Expectations who worked cruelly—not God. Her garish colors excited our flesh; His many-toned tints give dimension to our mind and heart. Her bold renderings keep our focus on things of earth; His careful, accurate perspective draws our eyes toward heaven. Her modernistic splashes disguise ugly world values; the precise insertions of grays and blacks by His eternal hand correctly present earth's darkness and make our soul yearn for His light.

My husband's grandfather, Bob Jones Sr., coined a succinct, accurate definition of success for a Christian: "Success is finding out what God wants you to do—and doing it." Beyond Scripture guidelines and the Holy Spirit's promptings, God indicates what He wants an individual to do largely by circumstances He ordains. To counteract a sense of missed success, then, we need to lock Lady Imagination's picture away in a closet and get on about the business of living our reality for the glory of God.

SATISFACTION

How many times have we responded to someone's questioning our momentary despondency with the age-old "I just feel . . ." When we experience that vague, oppressive sensation, it often has to do with *satisfaction*: a goal reached, comfortable circumstances, positive relationships. If one or more of those is deficient, we may hear the wind of emptiness. Why?

Let's think of feminine existence as having many compartments, with each marked incrementally from empty to full. Ideally we would keep each compartment's contents up to the top, creating satisfaction. As we eye that full line and see the contents fall short, we struggle with dissatisfaction. Winds blowing across the compartments create multiple tones and pitches. Low tones don't bother us overmuch; high-pitched whistling, though, causes unease and restlessness.

What are some of the less-than-full areas that typically serve as feminine trouble spots? Four come to mind:

- Rectified past
- Realized potential
- Relational positives
- Reproductive perfection

Consider typical expectations-versus-experience within those categories of desire.

Rectified past. Whatever lacks we may have known while growing up, we'd like them to be made right in our maturity, thank you very much! For instance, emotional scars should magically disappear, neglectful or abusive parents and siblings apologize, sinful personal choices of the past be wiped from memory.

Emotional wounds heal as we submit them to God, but the scars don't disappear. Neglectful or abusive parents and siblings may never apologize or even acknowledge their failures; instead they may continue or increase their hurtful treatment. Your own sinful choices, though cleansed by the blood of Christ, will ever remain lodged in your memory. Too, there may be lingering consequences from your earlier choices or experiences. Computer experts tell us that information entered in those modern technological wonders, though deleted, is never really eliminated from the machine's memory. The same is true of our human internal "hard drive."

Sighing winds blowing across the compartment labeled the Past need not mean either crimping or crippling—unless you choose to have it so. Instead, pain from yesterday actually can add a protective and useful dimension. Given into God's mighty hand, it can warn you to guard your vulnerable places, deepen your loving gratitude to God for your rescue, strengthen your desire to serve Him, and enrich your effective ministry to others.

The Bible presents a beautiful picture of that truth in Mary Magdalene. It's impossible to imagine the horrors of her life while she was indwelt by evil spirits. Christ's cleansing did not wipe out whatever physical batterings she had suffered. And today, hundreds of years since she walked the earth, the Magdalen stands as an example of Christ's ability to save "to the uttermost" and of a cleansed woman's tender, faithful discipleship.

Realized potential. The private, cherished sense of having within oneself a special capability will become reality: the internal artist, writer, speaker, entrepreneur, or executive will emerge and win acclaim.

There can be disappointment when a part of you that burns for expression never finds an outlet: the artistic soul doesn't get to paint, or design, or sing; the expressive heart doesn't experience the joy of writing; the entrepreneurial soul lacks opportunity to flourish; the born executive spends a lifetime in subordinate positions, carrying out mundane duties.

Whatever the area of interest, many Christian women feel they've missed out on something important. Such a person should consider two things. First, there's the distinction between public expression of a potential versus private expression. That very distinction may play a part in dissatisfaction. That is, the yearnings actually may be "I want to be recognized." Second, there's the matter of God's loving sovereignty. If your potential should be publicly expressed and recognized—according to His limitless wisdom—it would have been or it eventually will be. Let your heart rest quietly in that assurance.

The following simple but touchingly expressive poem "The Wild White Rose" by Ellen H. Willis deals with a heart's unreachables.

> It was peeping through the brambles that little wild
>   white rose,
> Where the hawthorn hedge was planted, my garden
>   to enclose.
> All beyond was fern and heather on the breezy, open
>   moor;
> All within was sun and shelter, and the wealth of
>   beauty's store.
> But I did not heed the fragrance of flow'ret or of tree;
> For my eyes were on that rosebud, and it grew too
>   high for me.
> In vain I strove to reach it through the tangled mass
>   of green,
> It only smiled and nodded behind its thorny screen.
> Yet through that summer morning I lingered near the
>   spot:
> Oh, why do things seem sweeter if we possess them
>   not?

My garden buds were blooming, but all that I could
see
Was that little mocking wild rose hanging just too high
for me.

So in life's wider garden there are buds of promise,
too,
Beyond our reach to gather, but not beyond our view;
And like the little charmer that tempted me astray,
They steal out half the brightness of many a summer's
day.
Oh, hearts that fail with longing for some forbidden
tree,
Look up and learn a lesson from my white rose and
me.
'Tis wiser far to number the blessings at my feet
Than ever to be sighing for just one bud more sweet.
My sunbeams and my shadows fall from a pierced
hand;
I can surely trust His wisdom since His heart I
understand.
And maybe in the morning, when His blessed face I
see,
He will tell me why my white rose grew just too high
for me.

Besides discerning between public and private personal desires
and resting in assurance of God's performing His intentions, we
who yearn for an unrealized potential should also make realistic
adjustments. Ongoing frustration is a sad waste of time, energy, and
opportunity. If you genuinely have a gift, why not express it right
now in your own "little" life circle? Pining for public use of a gift
actually may be abuse of that gift. We would be hurt if someone to
whom we gave a special present didn't open and use the gift. So too
God, Whose delight is to give to His children, expects His gifts to
be used. Each of us has daily opportunities to do so.

An artist? Your painting may never hang in an art show or a gallery—but you can create a unique bedroom for a child or a grandchild. You can express your artistry informally as you help friends decorate their homes. Surely there is need in your church or Christian school for your creative efforts. You needn't be a star in such projects—but your help can be vital.

A writer? Though your stories never see publication, why aren't you telling them to whatever children or teenagers occupy your circle? Do your part to revive the dying art of letter writing. You can have an effective writing ministry with pen and paper: use your creative gift to keep in touch with friends and family or to express concern and comfort to someone sorrowing, joy to someone celebrating, prayer for those discouraged. Contribute well-stated biblical positions in letters to the editor of your local newspaper. Or use your computer to create an exclusive compilation of stories for yourself and your family. A genuine gift for writing finds fulfillment in the doing—it doesn't demand publication by a vanity press.

A musician? Though the position of church pianist never opens to you, do you let that closed public door slam shut on your private musical expression? What wasted opportunities! No home of whatever size is richer than one filled with the sound of hymns, spiritual songs, classical and other good music. Any family is greatly benefited by having their tastes trained toward the best music and away from the ugly sounds of the world.

A public speaker? Your longing to instruct audiences can be soothed by a dose of reality: that woman you'd like to emulate or replace actually bears a burden of extra spiritual accountability and responsibility.

> My brethren, be not many masters [teachers], knowing that we
> shall receive the greater condemnation. (James 3:1)

Speaking opportunities daily present themselves. In ordinary conversations without trying to instruct others according to your superior knowledge or to inspire them by your elevated attainment, do speak those things that are burning in your heart. What a blessing are those women in my life who humbly, graciously, privately verbalize their spiritual understanding!

So your name and accomplishments aren't heralded by *Entrepreneur* magazine? Much more effective and important is the application of your gift within the walls of your home: design or refine domestic routines, invent labor-saving devices, help your children or friends establish an imaginative cottage industry. Use your visionary gift to inspire others; it may take as little as a suggestion, "Hey, why couldn't we . . . ?"

No business or professional group recognizes your management skills? Does that mean your talents are wasted? Not at all. They're just not rightly recognized and utilized—by you. Although God lovingly assigns women a role subordinate to men, He also gives them managerial abilities in life settings that call for their use. Consider, for instance, a single woman who commutes to her job, owns her car and her condo, is active in her church, and maintains a healthy friends-and-family network. Or think about the married woman whose husband travels in his business several times a month, whose thirty-year-old house has back and front yards to be maintained, whose children range in age from kindergarten through high school, and who teaches a ladies Sunday school class. How do women in such circumstances—or any number of other scenarios—successfully juggle all those balls of responsibility? By good management!

It's evident that a shift of focus needs to be made: from this unimportant little bit of earthly time to the unbounded expanse of eternity. No public or professional recognition can compare with the eventual commendation, "Well done . . ." spoken by Jesus Christ to His faithful servants.

Relational positives. We desire that acquaintances will be kind; friends loyal and supportive; relatives warmhearted; husband tender, intuitive, and adoring; and children grown to become our best friends.

God made us to be social creatures, and we yearn to translate "social interaction" as "altogether pleasant." Alas, life persistently fails to do so. Therefore, we may be wounded by people's unkindness, be devastated by friends' misunderstanding disloyalty, grit our teeth because relatives are obnoxious, ache for our husband's cherishing, or weep over estrangement from our grown children.

Interpersonal disappointments are reality for all of us because we live in a sin-cursed world. People are people—better at clogging the gears of social interaction than at meshing smoothly to meet our expectations. And of course not one of us is personally without fault in relationship problems.

The area of our personal relationships is a lifelong testing ground for our spiritual maturity. Therefore, a later chapter is devoted to relationships, making this brief mention here sufficient.

Reproductive perfection. Our expectation in this regard are many. At convenient times and manageable intervals children will be conceived, carried, and brought into the world. They'll have malleable temperaments and pleasing personalities. Each, of course, will be healthy and whole. Any difficulties they present in rearing will be of the cute type. Each will mature into an interesting individual, an admirable adult, a respected citizen, and a worthy Christian.

Had Eve not sinned, such hopes would be realized because we would experience the life perfection God intended. But she did, and we don't. It's in the "don't" that we suffer. The Bible states our case with wonderful directness.

Hope deferred maketh the heart sick; but when the desire cometh, it is a tree of life. (Proverbs 13:12)

Let's touch upon some of heart sickness we suffer by having experience destroy our expectations and ways to avoid or medicate the illness.

We come equipped with a deep-rooted desire for the fulfillment of motherhood, and we're talented in mentally designing and stage-managing that production. But what happens when reality's theater stages a different plot? You never marry. Or as a married woman you fail to conceive or miscarry repeatedly. Or you get pregnant on your honeymoon and produce child after child in quick sequence. Or one or more of your children has an iron will. Or you bear a child with a mental, emotional, or physical handicap. Or your daughter or son opts against doing right in favor of destructive, rebellious behavior. These examples can mean a wide range of disappointments and heart hurt. Emptiness' winds in some such cases may be near hurricane force. Beyond the basic need to abandon idealism, response and adjustment must correspond to the nature of the case. Let's go through the rewritten scenes and examine responses.

Adjusted Plot 1. An unmarried woman's innate maternal yearnings are bound up with her natural desire for marriage—a relational lack to be addressed in a later chapter. Just touching upon the subject here, however, God speaks marvelous consolation to a single woman's enforced childlessness through Isaiah 56:3b–5:

> Neither let the eunuch say, Behold, I am a dry tree. For thus saith the Lord unto the eunuchs that keep my sabbaths, and choose the things that please me, and take hold of my covenant; even unto them will I give in mine house and within my walls a place and a name better than of sons and daughters: I will give them an everlasting name, that shall not be cut off.

Of all childless people, a eunuch must be the most pitied, having been permanently denied reproductive ability by physical mutilation. Sovereigns of old routinely had servants made sexually dysfunctional to protect their royal harems. But ponder God's promise: even that forcedly single, childless person, if rightly related to God and living faithfully for Him, will have his name perpetuated in a manner and to a degree far greater than any physical lineage. The life ministries of single women can be full and rich: it is neither marriage nor children that create such fullness; rather, it is God Himself. More about this later.

Adjusted Plot 2. Though married, a woman may be unable to conceive or may have multiple miscarriages, wracking her emotionally. The physical unity of married love brings with it a strong desire for procreation. The Bible presents two women who dealt with childlessness, Sarah and Hannah.

Genesis presents the life of Sarah, the wife of Abraham. He was to be the great progenitor of God's chosen people, Israel. While she's honored as a princess and (ultimately) as an example of faith, in chapters 16–21 Sarah also demonstrates flawed womanhood. God revealed to Abraham early on that he would father a nation. Obviously, that meant his wife would be a key participant. But long years passed; years that confirmed Sarah's barrenness and moved husband and wife into old age. Disappointment and frustration outweighed Sarah's faith in divine fulfillment. So she decided to help God out: she persuaded Abraham to take her maid, Hagar, as a concubine. That plan fit with current cultural practice, but it didn't fit God's heart design. Oh yes, the "surrogate" pregnancy happened—but the price was high. The line begun by Hagar's son, Ishmael, became a permanent source of horrendous conflict that continues even into our modern age. Personally, too, Sarah's dream turned to nightmare as Hagar came to despise her mistress. That didn't please Sarah; she complained to her husband and treated Hagar so harshly that the maid fled into the wilderness. By trying to mold reproductive circumstances to her liking, Sarah displayed a huge failing of faith. Ultimately, God graciously put things back on track according to His timetable.

> And the Lord visited Sarah as he had said, and the Lord did unto Sarah as he had spoken. For Sarah conceived, and bare Abraham a son in his old age, at the set time of which God had spoken to him. (Genesis 21:1–2)

As she experienced Jehovah's fulfilled promise, Sarah's joy must have been tinged with shame for her earlier failure of faith.

First Samuel paints the portrait of another woman, Hannah. Like Sarah her predecessor, Hannah was unable to conceive. Worsening her barrenness was a rival wife in the household—Peninnah—who, in contrast to Hannah, was a baby factory and who flaunted her superior fertility. Poor Hannah was every bit as human and female as Sarah, but her response was vastly different. She didn't try to circumvent her situation by scheming. She didn't complain or whine. She didn't yammer at her husband, Elkanah. She didn't rail at sharp-tongued Peninnah. Though enduring tremendous emotional hurt, she took her woes only to God. In great agony of soul she petitioned Jehovah for the gift of fertility. During one of the family's annual pilgrimages to worship at Shiloh, Hannah's intense prayer was so marked that the priest, Eli, accused her of drunkenness. What a cruel blow for her aching heart! After Hannah explained to Eli the real reason for her behavior, he encouraged her to believe that her prayers would be answered. From that point on, Hannah activated her faith, conquered her emotions, and began living out her positive belief. Jehovah wonderfully rewarded her with a son, Samuel. The depth and breadth of Hannah's heart made her return to God the core delight of that heart as a thank offering.

Though her human self would have kept the boy in her arms, her spiritual self delivered him into God's arms. Hannah ultimately bore more children, but surely the truest, overflowing fullness she experienced was in seeing Samuel—the son of her initial triumph of faith—become a mighty prophet of Jehovah.

God tells us in Proverbs 30:16 that the barren womb is one of the four things that are never satisfied: the desire for reproduction is integral to our human physical and emotional structure. However, when reproduction is withheld, the Christian woman must throw herself in faith upon her heavenly Father's wisdom and love, surrendering her idea of "best" for His.

Adjusted Plot 3. Married women who are able to conceive and bear children still must jettison idealism. Otherwise it becomes a weight dragging your spirits downward and stalling spiritual progress. Realism recognizes that every child is born in sin and inevitably will demonstrate that fact. Imperfection may become evident early, and in something as basic—but distressing—as chronic colic or projectile vomiting. Mothers of such babies have tearfully told me of the horrendous pressures they experienced physically and emotionally. I can only imagine their exhaustion and worry. Or perhaps instead of physical anomalies a child possesses an iron will that lessens pleasure and intensifies pressure for the parents. Or he exhibits a forebear's fabled personality quirk, creating embarrassment and disciplinary challenges for the mother and father. Or severe physical or mental disabilities appear at birth, instantly increasing parental obligations. Or your daughter opts against doing right in favor of destructive, rebellious behavior. Or your son grows to an adulthood of financial irresponsibility, antisocial behavior, drunkenness or drug use, adultery, thievery, or homosexuality.

Whatever the child's unexpected characteristics or conditions, parenting must expand to meet the specific needs and provide special molding. In turn, God faithfully demonstrates that blessing and benefit come through His entrustment of that special child.

Instant acceptance, sweetness, and rejoicing are unrealistic expectations in parenting situations like some of those mentioned. Rather, mother and father will experience struggles, questionings, and tears. One of three basic choices must be made—escape, resentful adjustment, or genuine submission to God's will. In my own difficult maternal journey toward the latter, the Holy Spirit took me repeatedly to the powerful picture of Jesus Christ in Gethsemane. Bit by bit, kneeling there with Him in the darkness, I came to see my sacrifice of will as a microscopic thing when compared to His. And there the light of His love brought a rainbow to my tears. Some special, precious rainbows are seen only through tears.

> Weeping may endure for a night, but joy cometh in the morning.
> (Psalm 30:5)

For each child given into their care, Christian parents need God's daily enablement. They must exert consistent discipline of self and child, while demonstrating godliness in spirit and action— obviously, a huge order to fill!

Finally with regard to our offspring, we need to recognize that any child, no matter how carefully and prayerfully reared, may choose to rebel. When children go Satan's way instead of God's way, parents must trust their broken hearts and their children's broken lives into the Lord's hands. That takes intense prayer and determined faith. A blessed passage speaking encouragement for such heart-wounded parents is Jeremiah 31:16–17—

> Thus saith the Lord; Refrain thy voice from weeping, and thine eyes from tears: for thy work shall be rewarded, saith the Lord; and they shall come again from the land of the enemy. And there is hope in thine end, saith the Lord, that thy children shall come again to their own border.

❧ THINKING IT OVER ❧

There is no one, anywhere in the world, whose experience exactly conforms to hopes and dreams. The more determinedly we form and hold to our yearnings, the greater the difficulties we create for ourselves and for others. Ultimately, our energies are wasted, our talents unused, and God's intended purpose for our life thwarted. Instead, we need to acknowledge that our expectations have sprung from the dust around and within us; we need, rather, spiritual, scriptural expectation, which is hope anchored in the eternal.

> The hope of the righteous shall be gladness: but the expectation of the wicked shall perish. (Proverbs 10:28)

If we had this verse firmly fixed in mind and heart, we'd balk, blunder, or blubber less at the unexpected realities of life, wouldn't we? We would know security and peace in God's direction of our path. We would recognize that He directs in love and that His purpose is our blessing and His glory.

I pray that after walking through the instances of experiential challenge in this chapter and personalizing the principles as needed, you can more genuinely and joyfully give heart salute to Romans 8:28–29:

> And we know that all things work together for good to them that love God, to them who are the called according to his purpose. For whom he did foreknow he also did predestinate to be conformed to the image of his Son.

God's means of conforming us to Jesus Christ seldom reflect our expectations.

CHAPTER EIGHT

The Emptiness of Loss

Our nakedness at birth is an incontrovertible, accepted fact. But we desire life from that moment to fatten, clothe, and enrich us. Instead, passing years may strip away layer after layer of what we pursue, attain, and cherish. In some ways it's easier to handle a never-filled life compartment than one made suddenly empty of something or someone treasured.

There are, of course, many kinds of loss; we'll look into some of those that come into women's lives: loss of position, loss of a place, and loss of a person.

Loss of Position

An initial glance at the heading might bring to mind the difficulty of losing a job. But there are various "position losses" common to us. First and earliest would be loss of the position as family baby. While you may not remember the experience from your own childhood, you've no doubt witnessed it in your children or others' families. The baby of a family garners special attention, and even a very young child comes to treasure and expect that focus. Ah, but when another baby is born—what then? Suddenly things change: the position of baby has been taken over by another. Children unselfconsciously demonstrate their unhappiness over being disenfranchised: they may misbehave, sulk, weep brokenheartedly, or withdraw into compensational behaviors. Time and careful handling by the parents enable the replaced star to move into a different orbit.

A losable position one of us might experience in teenage years is that of leadership in elected or assigned places: high school, church group, sports, or music. When open competition is involved in some of those situations, there's not only disappointment, but a blow to one's pride as well. Such loss however can provide valuable character training for later, more serious losses.

Oddly enough, maturity sometimes finds a woman less able to handle a lost position than did childhood and teen years. *Maturity* may simply be a term meaning added years rather than advanced reasonableness and emotional control. That unflattering fact can be seen as lost positions cause resentment, bickering, and backbiting in our churches and Christian schools! Those negatives may be even stronger when children or grandchildren are the ones who fail to win or keep coveted positions. Such a negative response doesn't deserve sympathy or an attempt to help: it is, (or should be) instead, cause for shame, apologies, repentance, and change.

> Grudge not one against another, brethren, lest ye be condemned: behold, the judge standeth before the door. (James 5:9)

Of course there are position losses that cause natural, legitimate difficulties. Loss of a job upon which you're dependent for living expenses, for instance, is one of those. The uncertainty yawning ahead in a jobless future of course appears frightening. A wise first response in firing is careful analysis of your work performance: what caused the firing? Many people in our day lose jobs because of companies downsizing or making technological replacements. In other cases, employers fire those in their organizations who fail to perform or produce as needed. If your work performance was poor or your personality abrasive, admit the fault and determine to correct it in whatever future job you get.

Lost income is no light matter. There are, obviously, practical necessities such as job-hunting or retraining. But a Christian should also make spiritual responses. Rather than panic or angry complaints against unfairness, a quiet "Lord, what should I learn in this?" sets the stage for spiritual profit. When we ask that question and pursue its answer, the result can be soul riches. It's not unusual to hear stories of how God used job loss as a road sign to redirect someone's life route.

When we view it from a distance, we probably consider loss of position due to aging inevitable, but when it happens to us personally coolness ends and *retirement* or *replacement* becomes a hard-edged, cutting word. Whether the loss is in a secular profession or in the ministry, necessary adjustments bring multiple pressures. Changes often include tightening finances, relocation, and reordered priorities. Such major changes demand mental, emotional, and spiritual choices as well. Ideally, retirement's "release time" will enable more Bible study—a tightening grasp on God's hand. And the closer we draw to Him, the closer He draws to us.

Draw nigh to God, and he will draw nigh to you. (James 4:8)

And even to your old age I am he; and even to hoar hairs will
I carry you: I have made, and I will bear; even I will carry, and
will deliver you. (Isaiah 46:4)

A deepening relationship with Jesus Christ is the richest gold we
can know in our older years. It encourages genuine wisdom, sweetness of spirit, and growing compassion for others—all of which not
only make our own road pleasant but also smooth the pathway for
others. The opposite is equally true: self-focus will fill our mind
with uncertainties and our spirit with acid and will disconnect our
compassion. Obviously, the latter type of older person makes things
hard for everyone. As individuals we make choices that determine
whether retirement will be empty or full. Aging can find us echoing Solomon's wonderful soul expressions.

Now also when I am old and grayheaded, O God, forsake me
not; until I have shewed thy strength unto this generation, and
thy power to every one that is to come. (Psalm 71:18)

The hoary head is a crown of glory, if it be found in the way of
righteousness. (Proverbs 16:31)

Thou shalt guide me with thy counsel, and afterward receive me
to glory. (Psalm 73:24)

LOSS OF PLACE

Woman is a "nester." She delights to create a suitable home, and
she treasures its embrace. Man, conversely, thinks more practically
of home and its maintenance. So a change of place means different
things for a woman than for a man: it means loss for her (unless, of
course, she's making a "dream move" of some sort—and even then
there are emotional pangs involved). Moving for the woman isn't
difficult primarily in terms of physical labor; she's pulling up emotional roots—familiar, beloved surroundings, a sense of stability,
and the warmth of friendships. So how can she graciously respond

to a move that means so many negatives for her? By facing to the reality, focusing on whatever positives are involved, and determining not to look back with longing and regret.

We Americans are a highly mobile society. You probably can find illustrations among your own acquaintances of the hugely different feminine reactions to moving. As you review those—or perhaps remember moves you've made yourself—can you recognize the importance of mindset and spiritual focus? We can look upon a change of homes as either an end or a beginning, as an oppression or an opportunity. Our nests are not built of circumstantial twigs but of heart weaving. I have friends in both the military and ministry who demonstrate that fact. One will talk sadly of the hardness in frequent moves; another will tell of the challenge, benefit, growth, and opportunity involved.

If you and I could only be fully convinced of God's constant presence, interest, and working in our lives! But we often live as if He is somehow "better" or "closer" to us in one place than in another. A moving van can threaten our spiritual equilibrium. Should that be true?

God is near—always. He wants to hear us call. He delights to respond, and His supply is always sufficient. There need be no empty place—anywhere.

> Am I a God at hand, saith the Lord, and not a God afar off? (Jeremiah 23:23)

LOSS OF A PERSON

While relationships will occupy a later chapter, we'll concentrate here on bereavement, particularly noting the void of a marital loss through death or divorce.

Have you noticed in reading through the early chapters of Genesis the repeated phrase "And he died"? It appears so often that it becomes like a drumbeat: "And he died" . . . "And he died" . . . "And he died." Not only do we learn the life spans of the Jewish patriarchs but we're also powerfully reminded that no matter who or where you are, earthly life ends. The years of living may be many, or they may be few—but they're cut off. And each death means an empty place for those who cared for him or her. Inevitably, mortality takes its toll upon marital relationships. And in many ways loss through divorce has the effect of death as well.

Let's first explore general loss through death—loss that each of us must face early and late. Death is our enemy. Though its final rout is promised, its current ravages are agonizing.

Most of us probably can remember a death experienced while we were children. Most likely it was a grandparent who died. Much of our comprehension and response depended upon the words and behavior of the adults around us. I remember death's devastation when my maternal grandfather died.

Snapshots show that Grampa Callison was tall, thin, and rather homely. But to me he was—and remains—beautiful. He smelled of the outdoors—of Washington sunshine and apple trees. Laughter lurked in the twinkle of his eye and the up-tilt at one corner of his mouth. With his big, deep voice he loved to tease a grandchild and to sing funny story songs while he plucked his guitar. He created adventure by taking me in the rumble seat of his Model T Ford, running errands all over town. I first recognized vocal harmony and the beauty of hymns as he sang. I adored Bill Callison. But then he was gone. I was ten years old when I looked into his casket—and hated the monster Death for stripping my life of that important, beloved man. The reminders of heaven spoken by adults helped but did not destroy the awful ache; it faded gradually as it was washed with tears through succeeding days, months, and years.

I'm grateful today—as a grandmother—that the child Beneth was allowed grief's tears, not shamed for them or told that a Christian shouldn't weep.

In teenage years we may suffer the loss of a friend. Traffic accidents, disease, and war cut short the lives of many before they reach their twenties, and friends struggle in their loss. Though the born-again teenager can learn strong, lasting lessons, the emotional price of the teaching is high.

When we're adults, the loss of friends becomes more frequent. And each death leaves an empty place uniquely shaped by the individuality of that person. Such losses are not easy—nor should they be—if there was rich closeness in the relationship. As the pain of loss tempers, there is a lingering fragrance of that friend's touch upon our life.

At some point, too, comes the death of parents, whether with shocking suddenness or after slow, suffering disintegration. That loss has within it an incomparable dimension as we must break from the very root of our earthly existence. And the richer, more enjoyable the intergenerational relationship, the greater the tearing when it ends. Here, surely, may come the heart cry "But what will I do without him or her?" The death of my own mother, resulting from a car accident, gave rise to such a cry. Stripped of her warmth, her ready laughter, her utter belief in and encouragement of me, her patient listening and wise counsel, I felt devastatingly empty. Even as my tears fell, God spoke into that echoing void the truth of my need for greater dependence upon Him. And, graciously through the fifteen months of Mother's coma prior to her death, He completed the transfer of my emotional and spiritual umbilical cord to Himself. And oh, the filling! Mom had consistently urged me toward that transfer, but her absence enabled it.

Some experience the loss of a child in death. The shock of loss is great whatever the child's age and regardless of the circumstances. Here, too, there is a special character to the emptiness, reflecting the child's age, personality, familial integration, manner of death, and so forth. For a Christian mother, empty arms here can speak an abiding message of a full embrace There.

Let's think now in detail of losing one's husband through death or divorce. A wife who loses her husband may face especially great challenges in every area of her life—and all come while she's emotionally vulnerable. Consider some of those areas.

- Finances. Money matters that were her husband's domain open before her as a terrifying chasm:
  - Her husband's salary—her own full or partial support—is gone.
  - Financial records: Where are they? What do they mean?
  - Insurance: Is there any? How much, and how and when will it be available?
  - Indebtedness may suddenly come to light.
  - Bank account(s) may have been wiped out—by a deserting husband or by medical expenses.
  - Mortgage, various bills, and credit cards demand payment.
- Children. She must first help them through the loss of their father. Then their support, nurture, and education all descend upon her shoulders. If there are young sons, they present an extra dimension of parenting challenges.
- House. Can their home be kept, or must it be given up in the financial reshuffling? Where can or should they move? Household maintenance gets added to her many other responsibilities.

~ Car. Is it paid for, or does it still demand monthly payments? Does she know how to put fuel in it, let alone tend to its regular maintenance?

When divorce rather than death takes a husband, the difficulties worsen exponentially. The emotional shattering caused by betrayal and abandonment defies description. Property, alimony, and parental rights settlements very likely entail acrimony plus legal hassles and expense. Whereas death gives finality to the relationship, divorce marks a beginning—of extended, complicated interpersonal dealings.

The matters mentioned don't begin to describe the pressures and pain a woman may experience when she loses her husband. Yet they should awaken our sympathy and compassion. It's easy to imagine how emptiness may suddenly seem to make up her entire world.

The particular, individualized pain in empty places of loss varies greatly, with numberless details contributing. Yet, just as in every other life circumstance, the critical factor for a Christian woman is her response. Desperation, anger, fear, and bitterness defeat her and speak poorly of Christ to a watching world. Sorrow is inescapable, as is a struggle to regain one's emotional balance, mental clarity, and practical recovery. But comfort and help are available as we take our needs to the Savior. Even with streaming tears and aching heart, we can call out to God as did the psalmist.

> Save me, O God; for the waters are come in unto my soul. I sink in deep mire, where there is no standing: I am come into deep waters, where the floods overflow me. I am weary of my crying: my throat is dried: mine eyes fail while I wait for my God. (Psalm 69:1–3)

God's tender, effective filling with His comfort can be experienced only in sorrow's emptiness. The greater the loss, the richer and sweeter is our Father's outpouring of comfort.

> Blessed be God, even the Father of our Lord Jesus Christ, the Father of mercies, and the God of all comfort. (II Corinthians 1:3)

That marvelous comfort is a living, growing thing. It not only embraces us but ultimately moves our hearts and hands to reach out to share that embrace with others. That same passage in II Corinthians goes on in verse 4 to read:

> Who comforteth us in all our tribulation, that we may be able to comfort them which are in any trouble, by the comfort wherewith we ourselves are comforted of God.

THINKING IT OVER

We like to keep, and we hate to lose. That human trait operates at full intensity in each of us, and the more meaningful our possession, the more dreaded and difficult its loss.

The empty places addressed throughout this book do not result in lightening, that is, in the sense of a weight removed. Rather, whenever we lose something or someone of value, absence burdens our heart.

Long ago, when my husband and I lost our first baby to death within hours of his birth, someone sent me the following poem, "Lean Hard." Because God has used it repeatedly for my comfort and blessing, I want to share it with you.

> Child of My love, lean hard,
> And let Me feel the pressure of thy care;
> I know thy burden, child, I shaped it;
> Poised it in Mine Own hand; made no
> proportion

In its weight to thine unaided strength,
For even as I laid it on, I said,
"I shall be near, and while she leans on Me,
This burden shall be Mine, not hers;
So shall I keep My child within the circling
    arms
Of My Own love." Here lay it down, nor fear
To impose it on a shoulder which upholds
The government of worlds. Yet closer come:
Thou art not near enough. I would embrace
    thy care;
So I might feel My child reposing on My breast.
Thou lovest Me? I knew it. Doubt not then;
But loving Me, lean hard.

~Author Unknown

No poet, however talented in melodic expression, can attain unto God's own speaking:

Cast thy burden upon the Lord, and he shall sustain thee: he shall never suffer the righteous to be moved (Psalm 55:22).

CHAPTER NINE

Relational Emptiness

AGAIN, I CONSIDERED ALL TRAVAIL, AND EVERY RIGHT WORK,
THAT FOR THIS A MAN IS ENVIED OF HIS NEIGHBOR. THIS IS
ALSO VANITY AND VEXATION OF SPIRIT.

ECCLESIASTES 4:4

In the dawn of time the lushness of Eden failed to satisfy God's first human being, Adam. Why? He had an occupation—tending the garden, with all its shapes, colors, and abundant fruits. He had the presence of other creatures—the marvelous variety of birds, fish, and animals that moved fearlessly with and around him. He had the flawless setting of the garden itself—luxuriant plants of every kind, with the life-giving warmth of the sun and the earth's dew-refreshed ambience. Yet Adam's existence was not complete. His human frame had need of something else: companionship, communication, and completion through another like himself. In answer to that need, God created Eve.

We today, thousands of years beyond Eden, continue to reflect Adam's likeness in our need for relationships with other human beings. God made us to be social creatures. This area of life holds potential for varied empty places because pleasures or difficulties experienced within our relationships play strongly into our sense of well-being. Relationship was inherent in God's very creation of woman.

> And the Lord God said, It is not good that the man should be alone; I will make him an help meet for him. (Genesis 2:18)

Later, too, as He pronounced the curse upon Eve for her disobedience, God not only focused His punishment on her reproduction but also upon her relationships.

> Unto the woman he said, I will greatly multiply thy sorrow and thy conception; in sorrow thou shalt bring forth children; and thy desire shall be to thy husband, and he shall rule over thee. (Genesis 3:16)

By contrast, God directed Adam's curse toward masculinity's core—work.

> In the sweat of thy face shalt thou eat bread, till thou return unto the ground; for out of it wast thou taken: for dust thou art, and unto dust shalt thou return. (Genesis 3:19)

We can see these ongoing, divergent realities in our own lives and as they're played out among others. When is a man most miserable? When he's experiencing problems in his work. When does a woman feel most miserable? When she's faced with problems in her relationships. Let's look into some representative areas of relational challenges we women may experience, moving from casual to close.

EMPTY PLACES WITH ACQUAINTANCES

COWORKERS

A man's workplace well-being primarily springs from his skill and success in the job. A woman, however, is affected more by relational matters. She is keenly aware of and vulnerable to negative attitudes and actions in those with whom she works. Because so many women now work outside their homes, the possibility for relational difficulties has been greatly expanded. Empty echoes of hurt may rise from the following:

- Coworkers who talk about her behind her back or openly avoid and exclude her
- An employer who criticizes her work, refusing to be pleased; one who overloads her with duties yet doesn't acknowledge her contributions
- A fellow employee who is obviously jealous and attempts to outdo, undermine, or even replace her

A work week marked by people pressures added to the demands of the job itself can grieve a woman's spirit. It may, in fact, bring her to the point at which she'd label her entire work situation empty.

It may be that because we differentiate our nonchurch areas of life by the words *secular* or *workaday* we contribute to our own difficulty. Despite our general agreement that life doesn't divide into secular versus sacred, we nevertheless hold to the differentiation. So we may mind our scriptural *p*'s and *q*'s of attitude and behavior more carefully in a Christian setting than in an "ordinary" one. In truth, however, obeying Bible principles within a secular setting is perhaps even more important among unbelievers in terms of testimony for Christ. You and I live in a society that is increasingly pagan. Most people know nothing of the Bible other than that it's a book. Therefore, every born-again believer has both opportunity and responsibility to walk the Bible, allowing the unsaved to read its message in our life. The workplace—whether it be office, business, factory, commercial establishment, restaurant, or farm—with its built-in people pressures, provides a wonderful laboratory where Christianity can be put to the test.

The life of faith is meant to be down-to-earth and practical, seen in the fact that God repeatedly calls us to walk prudently in our everyday world.

> The prudent man looketh well to his going. (Proverbs 14:15)

When difficulties crop up with fellow workers, it's prudent to consider the basic facts of the job itself, and you in the job. These considerations may seem overly simple—but relational problems can be rooted in the soil of such facts.

The job itself

Type. It may fall anywhere within a broad spectrum: professional, technological, manufacturing, sales, financial, or whatever. Each type has its own particular built-in pressures.

Workplace structure. This may range from tightly compacted cubicles in a storefront office to off-site sales demanding only a weekly office meeting.

Pay schedule. Salary may be received weekly, biweekly, or monthly. It may be figured hourly or on the basis of commissions.

Organizational structure. There may be a clear pecking order with each person pigeonholed and labeled, or levels of responsibility may be indistinguishable except that all report to one manager. Procedures and expectations may take the form of a printed document, a training period, or a fifteen-minute introduction upon your arrival the first day.

Workplace atmosphere. Quiet may reign or music may be omnipresent. Conversation may be encouraged or frowned upon. Spiritual aura may range from blatant ungodliness to cool, professional secularism or to a ministry atmosphere.

Understandably, any aspect of the job can play into relationships within the workplace.

You in the job

First, you obviously need the job, or you wouldn't be there; hence, it's a means of supplying your financial needs. Do you appreciate it? Many today are unemployed and suffering tremendous financial difficulties as a result. Have you thanked the Lord for enabling you to work? Whether yours is a dream job or a drag, whether you like your fellow workers or not, we are told,

> In everything give thanks (I Thessalonians 5:18).

How different work—and relationships with other workers— can be depending on the presence or absence of gratitude. If, for instance, instead of gratitude you feel resentment because you have to work, each day on the job and every relationship therein has ten strikes against it.

Second, are you putting forth your best effort? Are you hard working, reliable, and honest in the work of your hands?

> The soul of the sluggard desireth, and hath nothing: but the soul
> of the diligent shall be made fat. (Proverbs 13:4)

Halfheartedness, laziness, or dishonesty in the workplace win their own—negative—reward from both employer and fellow workers.

Third, are you diligent in directing your spirit and your mouth— maintaining a pleasant spirit and speaking kind words?

> Servants [employees!], obey in all things your masters according
> to the flesh; not with eyeservice, as menpleasers; but in singleness
> of heart, fearing God. And whatsoever ye do, do it heartily, as to
> the Lord, and not unto men. (Colossians 3:22–23)

> The lips of the righteous know what is acceptable, but the mouth
> of the wicked speaketh frowardness. (Proverbs 10:32)

Now, having addressed those basics—which inevitably color every aspect of your work—we can move on to consider troubled work relationships. God provides a broad, strong platform for getting along in life's daily activities.

> If it be possible, as much as lieth in you, live peaceably with all men. (Romans 12:18)

There are peaceable responses to nonpeaceful work situations.

Let's first think about difficult fellow workers. They may be irritable, backbiters, sluggards, competitive, toadies, or any number of other hard-to-get-along-with types. Whatever the other person's attitude toward and treatment of you, your own temperament, personality, spirit, and responses will contribute to peace or war. Keeping that in mind, now consider your perspective regarding the other person. That perspective should be as positive as possible.

First, stop concentrating on the offender's flaws, and instead look for two things:

- His or her positive personal qualities
- Possible contributing factors in his or her life

Positive personal qualities. No one is all bad. Search out even the faintest glimmers of good in that pressuring person, then appreciate and commend him or her for those things. It is possible to "out nice" even the nastiest person. That God-enabled treatment of Mr./Mrs./Miss Nasty may ultimately be the magnet drawing him or her to inquire about its Source.

Contributing factors. The people with whom you deal each day are variously influenced and motivated. There may be difficult elements in that other person's being or life contributing to her unpleasant workplace persona. The possibilities are numberless, with some especially common—ill health, financial pressures, family difficulties, and personal insecurity or failure. Of course, if the unpleasant coworker is unsaved, there is no restraint of the Holy Spirit or instruction from the Word monitoring her actions and attitudes. Nor do Christians consistently live within genuine spiritual parameters.

Next, examine yourself as critically as you've been looking at the offender. How might your appearance, spirit, or actions affect other people? Even small things experienced day by day in close association in time-pressured settings can become like burrs and chafe to the point of causing a reactionary attack. Some possible "burrs" to look for in yourself are

- A lifted chin (nose in the air) or unconscious facial expression
- An attitude conveying superiority or grimness
- A martyr's air or inordinate mousiness
- An irritating habit such as chewing gum or cracking knuckles
- A voice that is phony sweet or fingernails-on-chalkboard shrill

Beyond self-scrutiny, God can also give you the grace to go to that difficult coworker to humbly inquire into the reason for his or her dislike or displeasure.

Debate thy cause with thy neighbor himself; and discover not a secret to another. (Proverbs 25:9)

Although the answer may be painful, you can benefit not only in the immediate situation but also in other areas of life as well. All of us have flaws that can adversely affect personal relationships.

EMPLOYERS

Generally speaking, an employer's spirit toward and treatment of a worker parallel the spirit and work output of the worker. The boss sees and is responsible for the overall picture in the workplace, whereas the employee carries responsibility for only one small portion. An efficient worker with a positive, cooperative spirit is a plus for the organization, and she also thereby makes the boss look good.

Wherever and for whomever you work, honestly examine yourself as an employee. The Bible holds up a measuring stick that can quickly reveal personal shortcomings.

> Servants, be obedient to them that are your masters according to the flesh, with fear and trembling, in singleness of your heart, as unto Christ. Not with eyeservice, as menpleasers; but as the servants of Christ, doing the will of God from the heart; with good will doing service, as to the Lord, and not to men. (Ephesians 6:5–7)

> Providing for honest things, not only in the sight of the Lord, but also in the sight of men. (II Corinthians 8:21)

> Servants, be subject to your masters with all fear; not only to the good and gentle, but also to the froward. (I Peter 2:18)

> And whatsoever thy hand findeth to do, do it with thy might. (Ecclesiastes 9:10)

Those principles apply to each of us in our employment situations—whether the setting be secular or Christian.

An added dimension that comes into play in Christian organizations are two wrong employee mindsets: feeling that careless work attitudes and slovenly production are acceptable and expecting a Christian employer to demonstrate bend-over-backward tolerance or extreme financial or medical undertaking. Scripture puts a quick end to both.

> Let as many servants as are under the yoke count their own masters worthy of all honor, that the name of God and his doctrine be not blasphemed. And they that have believing masters, let them not despise them because they are brethren;

but rather do them service, because they are faithful and beloved, partakers of the benefit. (I Timothy 6:1–2)

Finally, workplace difficulties must be bathed in prayer. God's help is essential in examining the overall situation, the other people involved, and self.

The Scripture and practical principles considered to this point address relatively ordinary workplace situations. There are instances, however, when a Christian employee must choose against the organization because she's asked or expected to dishonor God: drinking alcoholic beverages, gambling, lying, stealing, or committing sexual immorality. In such a situation Scripture obedience may well result in loss of the job. While completing this manuscript, I had a young woman tell of just such an experience. She had worked several years with a firm following her graduation from college, and she had advanced in the organization because of her diligence, talent, and efficiency. Her fellow workers' general mockery of her standards and exaggerated "carefulness" when near her were bearable—but problems went beyond that. Her boss made sexual advances in the office and asked her to "take business trips" with him. When she quietly but firmly rebuffed him, she was fired.

No workplace is perfect, and neither employers nor fellow employees are angels. In most cases, therefore, the Lord must enable you to endure: to bear difficulties patiently and to return love for mistreatment. Workplace relational difficulties present excellent opportunity to obey Christ's words recorded in Matthew 5:44—

But I say unto you, Love your enemies, bless them that curse you, do good to them that hate you, and pray for them which despitefully use you, and persecute you.

Our flawed flesh, if allowed its way in workplace difficulties, insures a troubling emptiness. However, wonderful fullness can be realized by denying the flesh and depending upon our Father's faithful supply.

> But unto every one of us is given grace according to the measure
> of the gift of Christ. (Ephesians 4:7)

I've had the joy through the years of meeting several women whose work situations were extremely difficult and their treatment unfair and downright cruel. In each case, however, these precious women accessed God's grace to a degree that can rightly be called heroic. Their hang-tough life testimonies in the workplace ultimately resulted in opened opportunities for the gospel, their vindication and advancement, and God's own punishment of the offenders.

EMPTY PLACES WITH FRIENDS

Friendships between women are multidimensional, deep, and lasting. When something happens to change or break friendship ties, a woman feels painful emptiness. As is often said, there is a fine line between love and hate. Women's friendships sometimes display the crossover. I've seen it happen—not just among unbelievers but among both lay and ministry Christians as well.

As a springboard for looking into the failures of others, it behooves us, first, to search out our own friendship factors.

> A man that hath friends must show himself friendly. (Proverbs
> 18:24)

Do you and I possess and demonstrate the positive friendship qualities we desire in others? Those qualities include warmth, concern, compassion, patience, kindness, and trustworthiness. The list is long, and we tend to recognize a missing or deficient item more easily in another person than in ourselves.

Now we can move on to think of the various difficulties that may occur in relationships:

- A slow cooling in a years-long friendship
- A sudden, unexplained rejection
- Loss of friendships due to long-distance moves
- A friend's failure in a time of one's special need
- Betrayal by publicizing confidences

Because of female emotional volatility, the road of women's friendships is fraught with rough and muddy places. Looking to the examples given, how can we wisely respond at difficult spots on that roadway?

A slow cooling? The longevity of the friendship should make it possible to approach the other person directly to ask if you have somehow inadvertently failed or offended her. If she replies in the affirmative, don't get defensive. Try to reach a point at which the two of you can calmly and openly discuss the problems. Perhaps, though, the cooling may be a natural result of altered life stages or changing personal interests or involvements. Sometimes the cooling can be reversed; in other situations we just need to accept the natural ebb and flow of life and the inevitable changes they bring.

A sudden, unexplained break? Again, the time factor would strongly play into the equation. A relatively brief friendship may end suddenly because of a major life change in one of the parties—a change she does not feel free to discuss. Or perhaps that other person has seen or sensed something in you—or in the chemistry of your relationship with her—that has called for a turnoff. One such factor often contributing to broken female friendships is one participant's too-strong approach. Too much closeness, too fast, too constant, too heart-exposing is not a healthy relationship; it's parasitic. Individual women also have different closeness needs in friendship relationships. Carefully analyze the entire situation before choosing whether to try talking through the matter, writing a brief, calm note of thanks for the past friendship and your willingness to discontinue it, or simply letting go silently as she has done.

Lost friendships due to a move? One party's change of locale will inevitably affect friendships that enjoy frequent communication and get-togethers. Distance-cut ties can be painful. In fact a sudden, total cutoff of a supportive friendship network can deplete a woman's sense of well-being. It's wise, therefore, to bridge the separation as much as possible. That might include a going-away party with all your group or individual goodbye lunches or coffees. Either way, the participants should not be loath to speak the sadness of their hearts—perhaps with tears. After all, that honesty of expression is one of genuine friendship's great treasures. Once the move has taken place, don't hesitate to establish some means of continuing communication—writing, calling, and e-mailing. As time passes, the contacts probably will decrease in frequency, but they need never stop completely. One of the blessings of genuine friendships is their ability to impart unique heart warmth even in small, infrequent doses.

A friend loveth at all times. (Proverbs 17:17)

Friends' hearts can sense one another's needs to an unusual degree. Most of my dearest friends live far away—yet over and over again I've experienced special comfort or encouragement in times of need without my ever having mentioned the need. Godly friendships are a gift that should not be undervalued or neglected.

A friend's failure in the time of your need? There can be great hurt in such an experience. Be careful, however, lest you concentrate exclusively or with undue intensity upon the incident: both the failure and the pain will be magnified out of all proportion. Rather than wallowing in blame and disappointment, look at the incident realistically. Had you communicated your need, or its exact nature? We women sometimes unfairly expect others to "key in" on our internals simply through sympathetic understanding. Was your expectation of her response or help reasonable? The intensity of our own experience in the incident can blind us to a friend's limited ability to provide the assistance we crave. Determine to put as good a face upon the situation as possible. Remind yourself of the many positive things your friend has done in the past. Give her the benefit of the doubt by refusing to think that she intentionally hurt you. Honesty surely would make any of us admit that somewhere, sometime, somehow we, too, have failed a friend in a time of her need.

Betrayal by publicizing confidences? That's a sure weapon of destruction in friendships, and betrayal's pain is real. In such a case, though, let the experience teach you the lesson that it's always safest to keep your own counsel. We women seem to have a built-in desire to share our heart with friends. But any such confidence presents an opportunity for purposed publication or slip-of-the-lip revelation. Your friend may have had no intention to pass along what you'd confided. But the pleasure of "inside" knowledge plus simple enjoyment of talking among women can effectively blow the lid off secrecy's container. No matter how or why the confidential information is published, it is a betrayal of trust. But resentment toward your unfaithful friend will only worsen your hurt. Forgive her—quickly and completely. But do call a halt to sharing further confidences with her. She has proven that your relationship should be trimmed. God speaks clearly about such a "friend" in Proverbs 11:13—

> A talebearer revealeth secrets; but he that is of a faithful spirit concealeth the matter.

Christian friendships are beneficial not only in what they add to our lives. They may also reflect our spiritual reality and depth. Because women's friendships involve close and important attachments, they present a point of vulnerability. Surely we've all seen instances in which a friendship somehow becomes detrimental—either in its ongoing intensity or complications or through its destruction. Take a moment right now to consult the barometer of each of your own friendships by posing the following questions:

- Does this friendship encourage my spiritual growth and hers?
- Does fondness for my friend make me tolerate unbecoming speech or behavior in her?
- Is this friendship bond so important to me that it threatens to outweigh ethical considerations and biblical principles?

Before leaving the topic of friendship, there is yet another source of emptiness within its sphere that should be addressed: lack or scarcity of close friendships. Many times this condition exists because of leadership or formal ministry. If you're the supervisor or boss, the boss's wife, or the pastor's wife, chances are strong that one of two things is true with regard to friendships:

- Some will seek to be your friend for sycophantic, self-elevating reasons.
- Some will stand apart from friendship with you because of your position.

Whatever the contributing factors, the resulting hard-to-handle friendship zone can create an empty place of loneliness. A woman's yearning to have a close friend can grow to immense proportions, and her heart cry "I need a friend!" can echo in every area of her life.

God sees fit to allow close friendships in some cases of leadership loneliness—usually with someone outside the group of followers (employees or congregants): for example, preachers' wives' close bonds are with other preachers' wives rather than with their church women. In professional situations close friends can be found outside one's circle of employees. Sometimes, however, no matter what or where her life may be, a woman may be denied bosom buddies. If that's true of you, has God short-changed you? Has He failed in His promise to supply your needs? Not at all. He has, in fact, presented a wonderful opportunity. As you yield that unmet longing to the Lord, and demonstrate satisfaction with whatever more casual friendships mark your life, God Himself will move in to fill the empty place. Three Bible characters come to mind. Although they're not women, these individuals stand as magnetic examples for you and me.

The patriarch Abraham, called out of his own land and from among his own people, faithfully undertook a God-ordained journey to an unknown land. As we read of him, his aloneness is evident—even in his marriage as Sarah failed to encourage his faith. Although at times his sense of isolation must have been great, it was offset. As we learn from James 2:23, he was called the friend of God. James points us to the supreme moment of that friendship: Abraham's spiritual obedience despite his natural desire and affection when he laid his son Isaac upon the altar of sacrifice. Abraham chose to move toward God rather than remain in his native land or retain his precious, miraculous paternal relationship with Isaac. And God showed Himself to be the All-Sufficient Friend.

The second example is Moses—that towering leader of Israel as the people came out of Egyptian captivity and moved toward the Promised Land. The million-plus people following him certainly didn't show themselves friendly! Nor did his siblings, Aaron and Miriam, exemplify faithful familial bonding. But Moses didn't whine and complain of loneliness. He simply moved forward, doing the job to which God had called him. And God Himself moved in to fill the void of human friendship. Scripture tells us that in instance after instance,

The Lord spake unto Moses face to face, as a man speaketh unto his friend (Exodus 33:11).

And finally, consider David. He's particularly interesting in the matter of friendship because of the unusually strong bond he had with Jonathan in their youth. Once death took Jonathan, however, David had to move forward into and through his kingship over Israel alone. His sense of isolation comes through clearly as we read many of his psalms. He experienced enmities from both outside and within his own house. But, like Abraham and Moses, David turned to that One Who is the "friend that sticketh closer than a brother." Though Scripture makes it clear that David was far from perfect, his heart consistently yearned toward God. And that mighty Friend proclaimed him to be a man after His own heart.

Whatever relational difficulty we may experience with friends, we should allow the inevitable failures in earthly bonds to renew and increase our gratitude for the unbreakable, never disappointing eternal bond God has allowed us to have with Him. Our heavenly Father proclaims His constant nearness to us—yet His gracious heart allows you and me the choice for or against the strength of that bond.

Draw nigh to God, and he will draw nigh to you. (James 4:8)

As in the case of the three men whose lives speak to us from the pages of Scripture, we need to know assuredly that close human friendship is a want—but our need is intimate, vital friendship with our Lord and Savior, Jesus Christ.

THINKING IT OVER

The world outside the doors of our home offers constant, multiple opportunities and challenges in relationships. Whether our contacts with individuals are momentary or extended, a God-ward mindset should color our attitudes and actions toward them. Rough relational places are not meant to defeat us. Instead, like sandpaper, they can smooth some of our many bumpy, bristly places. In all our human relationships we have opportunity to demonstrate our heavenly relationship. The apostle Paul frequently connected his social interactions to his spiritual testimony.

> But we were gentle among you, even as a nurse cherisheth her children: so being affectionately desirous of you, we were willing to have imparted unto you, not the gospel of God only, but also our own souls, because ye were dear unto us. (I Thessalonians 2:7–8)

And when people failed him utterly, Paul forgave them, relying upon and rejoicing in the greater relationship.

> At my first answer no man stood with me, but all men forsook me. I pray God that it may not be laid to their charge. Notwithstanding the Lord stood with me, and strengthened me. (II Timothy 4:16–17a)

CHAPTER TEN

EMPTINESS
WITHIN FAMILIES

IN THE DAY OF PROSPERITY BE JOYFUL, BUT IN THE DAY OF
ADVERSITY CONSIDER: GOD ALSO HATH SET THE ONE OVER
AGAINST THE OTHER, TO THE END THAT MAN SHOULD FIND
NOTHING AFTER HIM.

ECCLESIASTES 7:14

Every shade of relational reality can be found within the walls of
home. Great joy comes from those that are bright but immense pain
from the brooding hues.

SIBLING DIFFICULTIES

Ideally, brothers and sisters would have warm, enjoyable personalities and would be kind, loving, thoughtful, and undertaking. Real
life may find them personally obnoxious, unkind, cold, thoughtless,
and unconcerned. Difficult relational situations could include the
following:

- General coolness and disinterest in being together
- Open jealousy and rivalry

- Gossip and put-downs
- Festering resentment and dislike
- Areas of strong, distinct disagreement and contention

However blood bonds may cool, women suffer from the cold. And because of the contrast between the bond's physical reality versus its emotional attributes, discomfort can be constant and strong—a hurtful empty place.

Each step closer in relational ties means the possibility for deeper hurt. Let's explore the listed examples.

There is a general coolness and disinterest in being together. Many factors may enter into a sibling's isolation from the family—none of which is admirable. It may be that self-focus and laziness make them bypass opportunities to gather. Or some petty personal animosity may keep them away. Or pride may be the barrier—they consider themselves richer, more educated, more socially elevated, and so "above" the rest of the family. Or a spiritual chasm of various sorts may make them uncomfortable among their siblings. Anchor your response to such siblings by realizing that although they're creating an empty place for you and others in the family, they're most of all cheating themselves. They're more to be pitied than resented.

Whatever reason they may state or harbor, don't allow your response to exacerbate the problem. And don't give up on them. Pray for the Lord to heal the break, and let your spirit, words, and actions consistently be magnetic rather than retaliatory.

There may be open jealousy and rivalry. This can be a long-standing source of hurt. Any number of things can become the focus of jealousy. A brother or sister may resent and envy your appearance, gifts, place in life, marital state, bank account, and so forth. The antagonistic spirit of jealousy is that person's fault, not yours—unless somehow you're communicating competition with or superiority over him or her. Ask God to help you search out and rid yourself of any such spirit. At the same time, prepare for possible expanded difficulties resulting from the presence of envy.

> For where envying and strife is, there is confusion and every evil work. (James 3:16)

And through all, determine to return kindness for spitefulness. You may experience gossip and putdowns. Difficult to handle even in casual relationships, these are much more so when the offenders are brothers and sisters. Damage to your reputation through a brother's or sister's gossip can be especially great, since hearers tend to think an "insider's" knowledge is accurate. As in all other gossip situations, it's impossible to correct resulting wrong impressions. Rather than a crusade of verbal denials, the most effective response is to live a daily contradiction of the spurious accusations. And though the sibling putdowns are deeply painful, they need not destroy. Balm and blessing can be found in the Scripture assurance—

> Thou shalt hide them in the secret of thy presence from the pride of man: thou shalt keep them secretly in a pavilion from the strife of tongues (Psalm 31:20).

There may be festering resentment and dislike. Strongly contradictory to the desirables in sibling relationships, these negatives probably have roots reaching back into your childhood together, with unfairness—real or imagined—a major factor. For instance, in a home where parents practice favoritism, children outside its warm embrace suffer the cold. They likely will react against the favored one(s). Or perhaps school days find siblings unfairly compared by teachers, and the "pet" factor rankles. In other cases a brother or sister just may seem to have been born with a negative mindset, and siblings make especially handy dartboards for such folks.

Hurtful as these antipathies are, the resentful sibling's attitudes lie beyond your corrective ability. Your own spirit does lie within your control, however, and Scripture obedience will find you counteracting the infection of antipathy with the ointment of kindness.

A brother offended is harder to be won than a strong city: and their contentions are like the bars of a castle. (Proverbs 18:19)

She openeth her mouth with wisdom, and in her tongue is the law of kindness. (Proverbs 31:26)

You may have areas of strong, distinct disagreement and contention. Arguments and occasional physical battles often mark sibling relationships in childhood. Rightly handled by the parents, those are fleeting and give way to affectionate appreciation for one another. On the other hand, though, maturity may instead produce strong opposites through chosen loyalties: religious, political, moral, athletic, and so forth. Loyalties involve emotion; passions many times run high and tempers may become explosive.

A fool's lips enter into contention, and his mouth calleth for strokes. (Proverbs 18:6)

Argumentation seldom shakes anyone's loyalties, however misguided they may be. It's far wiser, therefore, to agree to disagree and avoid discussing explosive topics. Unsaved or spiritually disobedient siblings should of course be a constant prayer burden on your heart.

Whatever the difficulties experienced with brothers and sisters, as a Christian you need to be loving, consistent, and patient. At every point ask the Lord to work in the hearts of your siblings—and in your own heart. He can give you guidance and enablement for your testimony in spirit, word, and deed.

EMPTY PLACES WITH PARENTS

Home heritage is a tremendous part of our existence. It not only determines our structure genetically but also molds our childhood and leaves lifelong marks upon us. While no home is perfect because of the imperfect people who form it, there is a wide range of emotional, mental, and spiritual atmospheres—from warm and nurturing to icily or hotly destructive.

Probably there are few if any who can look back upon their childhood home without recognizing at least some small lack. For many, though, that backward glance brings an immediate, painful sense of emptiness. The hollow place may reflect just a small but regretted parental misunderstanding of one's basic makeup, or it may seem a deep, dark cave formed by outright rejection or cruelty.

Parent-child relationships offering the greatest difficulties and sense of emptiness are those in which animosities remain alive and fester into adulthood.

Parental mistreatment or rejection in the past can have carryover effects in the present. When one's childhood home was a hurtful place, continuing pain and relational unease will reflect the severity of the mistreatment as well as the intensity of present complications. In the case where a father sexually abused his daughter, she as an adult will not only have to deal with her own scars but she'll also necessarily guard her children against possible similar mistreatment.

No matter how you were hurt by your parents, it is essential that you forgive them.

> And when ye stand praying, forgive, if ye have ought against any: that your Father also which is in heaven may forgive you your trespasses. But if ye do not forgive, neither will your Father which is in heaven forgive your trespasses. (Mark 11:25–26)

Christ's command is clear, and there is no exception clause. Forgiving parent-inflicted wounds can be extremely difficult—but unforgiveness not only harms your adult relationship with your father and mother but also puts a barrier between you and your heavenly Father. We who have experienced devastating parental treatment must put aside all delaying, deadening tendencies: lack of understanding, desire for reckoning, sense of victimization, wanting an apology. Instead, we must access the all-enabling grace of God and let Him prove in and through us that nothing is too hard for Him.

Bruising childhood experiences demand God's healing. Because my book *Mount Up on Wounded Wings* deals with overcoming hurtful home wounds, we'll not go further into the subject here.

PARENTS' DIVORCE

When parents divorce, children are cut loose from their emotional moorings and suffer tremendous hurt. If antagonism and bitterness continue between the parents, with each trying to shift blame and win sympathy, the relationships suffer ongoing abrasion.

A sad characteristic of our modern times is the tolerance Christians have for divorce. The Bible makes it plain that God looks upon marital dissolution very differently.

> Because the Lord hath been witness between thee and the wife of thy youth; against whom thou hast dealt treacherously: yet is she thy companion, and the wife of thy covenant. And did not he [God] make one? Yet had he the residue of the spirit. And wherefore one? That he might seek a godly seed. Therefore take heed to your spirit, and let none deal treacherously against the wife of his youth. For the Lord, the God of Israel, saith that he hateth putting away. (Malachi 2:14–16)

Our tolerance of what God hates carries with it a heavy price—a price borne mostly by the children of the broken home.

While modern sociologists have held that divorce has little effect upon children if parents handle the breakup "maturely," time has proved otherwise. A home is a unique, unified group of people, and when the strategic foundational element in the entity rips, suffering is inescapable. Children have their sense of security badly shaken, and they may blame themselves for somehow contributing to the dissolution. Fears set in: uncertainties that not only affect their present but their future as well. Current trends toward ever-later marriages in the younger generation reflect such fears. Many children of divorce feel that parental divorce makes the child unfit for marriage at all or dooms him or her to marital failure.

If you are a child of divorce, you might personally attest to the above statements and perhaps add a lengthy addendum. The point is, however, a child of divorce needs to put behind her whatever negative effects may linger in mind and heart so that she can move forward positively herself and have a positive life ministry as well. That means abandoning lingering resentments toward your mother or father, repenting of anger felt toward God for having let it happen, and relinquishing fears. It may also mean asking forgiveness of your parent(s) for earlier wrong reactions and implementing measures for improved relationships with all who are involved.

PARENTS' REMARRIAGE AND ATTEMPTED BLENDING OF FAMILIES

If one or both divorced parents remarry, a child may feel betrayed or repulsed personally and in behalf of the original marriage partner. Children of divorced parents face multiple adjustments that are difficult in themselves. When one or both parents choose new marriage partners, another whole world of difficulty opens to the offspring. Step-relatives must then be accommodated as a new family is formed. That blending may require the sacrifice of some emotional dimension in terms of ties with loyalty to the birth parent or blood siblings.

The "new" parent also will bring a different personal contribution to the family equation, and his or her parenting methods and expectations may be wholly unlike the original pattern. Children of that newcomer will likewise have a dissimilar life history, as well as their own emotional scars from home breakage.

Fleeing from or refusing to accommodate the new situation can only worsen it. A child of whatever age is wise to respond, instead, in such a way that the new relationships and the restructured family work as smoothly as possible despite the inevitable difficulties.

Ideally, everyone concerned will do his or her part to create a formula for success. More realistically, however, there probably will be at least one who has not overcome pain, confusion, or denial. In the latter case those with the more positive, Scripture-prompted attitude must pray and work even harder—ministering to that deeply wounded one and nurturing the fragile thread of unity.

PARENTAL INTRUSION INTO ADULT CHILDREN'S LIVES

Parents sometimes fail to recognize and adjust to the independence of their married children. They hover over them, wanting to know what's going on in minute detail, wanting to talk or visit over-often, trying to give direction in decisions, offering advice on anything and everything. Such parental smothering presents unnecessary difficulties for those establishing their new home and life together.

I recently heard a story of horrendous parental intrusion. The parents of a young wife insist that each morning when her husband goes to work he must drop off the girl to spend the day with them. Too, the controlling father not only continues to act as his daughter's authority but also bosses his son-in-law. Yet these parents claim to be Christians! Somehow, they and other smothering parents are managing to ignore God's own description of marriage.

> Therefore shall a man leave his father and his mother, and shall cleave unto his wife; and they shall be one flesh. (Genesis 2:24)

Parents who fail to cut the apron strings from a child when he or she marries do the offspring, the mate, and the new marriage relationship an immense disservice. That particular parental practice often reflects an unacknowledged fact: their own marriage is weak. That is, one or both parents have failed to build and maintain a solid, warm, personally fulfilling and God-honoring marital unity. Hence he, she, or they have transferred the intense emotional attachment they owe one another to their child(ren). While the parents' inadequate marriage is pitiable, it must not be allowed to drain health from the children's marriage.

Parents maintain apron strings in a number of ways.

Too-frequent communication. Making contact daily is overage. It draws essential prime communication away from the child's mate.

Maintaining a room at home for the child. Such action says, in effect, "Here is where you belong. You can always run back to us."

Financial support or rescue. Either of these damages the couple's autonomy. Slipping extra cash to your daughter infers her husband's inadequate financial support. Providing monetary rescue when the young couple suffers from unwise spending short-circuits important lessons they need to learn. The area of finances is a prime opportunity for God to show Himself real to the younger generation as He teaches them the importance of faithfully giving back to Him and the necessity for financial self-discipline.

Over-togetherness for holidays and vacations. Expectations and demands of togetherness bind the young couple to parental traditions rather than allowing them to establish their own new ones and nurture their own new family unit. With Mom and Dad picking up all or part of the vacation tab and drawing everyone back to the home place for holidays, "good times" may come to mean only—or primarily—those spent with the older generation. It's a case of too much too often—overwhelming the young family's needed autonomy.

If you are one of the older generation and recognize some of your practices in the above descriptions, untie the strings. You and your husband are the God-ordained unit in your own marriage; children are on loan from Him to be reared and released into God-reliant, faithful adulthood.

If you're in the younger generation and you're experiencing the other end of the parental apron strings, gently petition and act for their loosening. The bulk of that transaction should be handled by the blood child of the offending parents; otherwise in-law resentment can flare and grow to a destructive flame. In most cases kind, restrained, but forthright discussion should sufficiently motivate positive change. But in other instances improvement will come only if the younger couple moves away from the older one.

PARENTS' DISINTEREST IN ADULT CHILDREN'S LIVES

Opposite to the above instances of smothering, some parents behave as if a child's marriage marks the end of parental involvement entirely. These parents fly off into their own, separate orbit. They're uninterested in the young couple's life, avoid contact and communication, and shrug off appeals for assistance or advice. In such cases, the children feel abandoned.

Near-complete severing of ties between generations renders grown children a puzzling hurt. Each of us knows instinctively that the parent-child relationship, though going through different stages, is meant to be lifelong. Too, we sense that children's adulthood provides opportunity for expanded relationship: a special intergenerational friendship. Parents and children alike are cheated when that opportunity gets short-circuited.

The most probable motivating factor in parents' jettisoning their adult children is selfishness: the feeling that they've done enough and spent enough rearing the children. They claim the golden years as their inalienable right. The resulting unnatural alienation, however, actually reduces the gold from twenty-four karat to ten karat. It also puts tin into their children's lives.

Children who experience parental detachment must guard against resentment and, by God's enabling, demonstrate one-way loving concern. The strategic investment of prayer for the situation can ultimately bring improvement to the relationship as God moves into the equation.

Whatever the specific parent-child relational difficulties may be, the Lord holds out the wonderfully calming, strengthening of His hand and heart in Psalm 103:13—

> Like as a father pitieth his children, so the Lord pitieth them that fear him.

FILIAL DIFFICULTIES

Relational bruises aren't limited to those felt by children. The opposite is often true, as well; parents may experience hurtful empty places due to their children's attitudes and actions. Relational hurts typically come with the child's adulthood and independence. For Christian parents, of course, the greatest pain comes from a son or daughter's rejection of a spiritual heritage. The rejection may take one of many forms from spiritual disinterest to gross immorality to Satanism. The greater the distance from home training and parental hopes, the worse the heartache experienced by a godly father and mother. Relational strains may result from the following:

Their spiritual rebellion and ungodly lifestyle. For parents who love the Lord, there is no deeper hurt, no greater heartbreak than that of offspring who reject the light and choose paths of darkness. A natural human reaction to unspeakable pain is to strike back at or separate from the hurter. But those natural reactions most likely will only add to the difficulties; reaction meets with reaction, hardening attitudes, deepening wounds, and putting relationships into a downward spiral that creates an unbridgeable chasm. Nor can such reactionary behavior act as a magnet to draw the child back to God or reflect His heart of love and longsuffering.

Godly parents of course cannot condone a rebel's choices. While hating the child's sin, they must love the child. Even in imagination that critical counterbalance looms as an enormous challenge; in actuality it must appear to be impossible. Nevertheless, steadfast parental love forms the most crucial link, humanly speaking, in the chain God can use to draw the prodigal to salvation and restoration.

As in the case of the psalmist David and the multiple instances of heartbreak he experienced through his children, today's hurting parent can have eyes and heart lifted heavenward by God's Word.

> The Lord also will be a refuge for the oppressed, a refuge in times of trouble. And they that know thy name will put their trust in thee: for thou, Lord, hast not forsaken them that seek thee. (Psalm 9:9–10)

Their refusal or failure to be independent and self-supporting. Independence is the natural goal toward which parents bend their efforts throughout the years of child rearing. But a growing number of adult children either don't leave or return to their parents' home. Prolonged dependence drains the relationship between the generations and may strain the parents' marriage bond as well.

While in most cases home-clinging indicates a flaw in the child, it also signals weakness in the parents. "When you grow up and move out on your own" should have been an underlying parental theme throughout the child-rearing process. In the teen years practical preparation should have been made: teaching of financial realities, individual responsibility, a solid work ethic, self-discipline, and a standard of personal excellence in all. The natural sequel to such training is the child's independence. Making the sequel reality may demand the parents' tough love. Allowing continued dependence is unhealthy for everyone involved.

If some unforeseen, unavoidable occurrence draws an offspring back into his or her parents' household, the temporary nature of the arrangement should be stressed at the outset, and the child's diligent, consistent efforts toward that goal carefully monitored.

There are, of course, situations in which the general principles cannot be applied because of the child's physical, mental, or emotional debilitation. In such cases, parents will be called upon for heroics that have nothing to do with sports contests or medals. They deserve our highest respect, our thoughtful concern, our prayers, and our helping hands.

Their marriage to someone unpleasant. A final type of filial wounding comes when a child's marriage brings into the family a son-in-law or daughter-in-law who resents the original home and reacts against it. The resentment may be expressed by emotional coldness or by the severity of avoidance and lying gossip.

Just as the parents' marriage is crucial in the tenor of children's lives, so children's marriages negatively or positively affect family relationships. That ever-so-sweet Christian girl can turn out to be a shrew after she has successfully captured your son. The great youth group star may become a flaming comet or a cold, dead asteroid after he pulls your daughter into his galaxy.

Family ties are naturally strained when added members subtract in spirit. I weep with and pray for my friends who endure that unhappy reality. And I salute their kind, godly responses in the face of harsh, insulting behavior and their prayerful intercession for the unworthy daughter- or son-in-law as well as for the suffering child.

Looking back over the various relational situations presented in these chapters, there comes to my mind a seriocomic observation heard repeatedly through the years: "Ministry would be wonderful, except for the people." "Teaching is a great profession, apart from dealing with the students."

Those could further be expanded to apply to the present topic: "Life would be great—if it just weren't for people."

But of course people surround each of us—and relating to them creates experiences that range from delightful to dreadful. Delightful of course poses no problem. But as we move along the relational scale toward dreadful, challenges abound.

In my own pressured relationships the Lord has brought two Scripture passages into sharp, instructive focus, and it's His Word that will end this discussion.

> Grudge not one against another, brethren, lest ye be condemned: behold, the judge standeth before the door. (James 5:9)

> Follow peace with all men, and holiness, without which no man shall see the Lord: looking diligently lest any man fail of the grace of God; lest any root of bitterness springing up trouble you, and thereby many be defiled. (Hebrews 12:14–15)

✤ THINKING IT OVER ✤

Our human hearts naturally long for the enrichment of positive human relationships. As noted in the opening of chapter 9, God created our relational dimension and called it good. Moreover, it is within that very dimension that God and man must meet. The marvelous, only, true, ever-living Creator God is not a metaphysical concept; He is a Person. And in His divine Personhood He seeks relationship with you and me. What an astounding reality! He clearly demonstrated that desire in Eden until the awful moment when, because of human choice, God's visit to the garden brought forth this heartrending call "Where art thou?"

Humankind had chosen sin—thus making continued relationship with God impossible. Still, Love continued to desire relationship with His creature, man. That desire was so strong that He spanned the immeasurable chasm of demanded condemnation—spanned it with the cross on which He shed His sin-cleansing blood.

When you and I meet with difficulties of any sort in our personal relationships and suffer because of them, we can be calmed and encouraged by moving our gaze from our own experience to that far greater one of God's as recorded for us. There in Eden He knew betrayal of the worst sort—yet all His response was in the love of His heart and for the good of the betrayers. For thousands of years His longsuffering has stated, "But my hand is stretched out still." And of course its ultimate expression was in Jesus, the Lamb of God, dying on Calvary for His creatures, who cursed and mocked Him. In view of such overwhelming reality, our thorny relationship experiences shrink to more realistic proportions, and our determination to respond correctly is strengthened.

Whatever our horizontal relational difficulties, our remembrance of and concentration upon our vertical relationship is essential—and therein will we be filled.

> Blessed is the man whom thou choosest, and causest to approach unto thee, that he may dwell in thy courts: we shall be satisfied with the goodness of thy house, even of thy holy temple. (Psalm 65:4)

CHAPTER ELEVEN

ROMANTIC EMPTINESS

THE WIND GOETH TOWARD THE SOUTH, AND TURNETH ABOUT
UNTO THE NORTH; IT WHIRLETH ABOUT CONTINUALLY, AND
THE WIND RETURNETH AGAIN ACCORDING TO HIS CIRCUITS.

ECCLESIASTES 1:6

Probably, for women, the most troublesome (or at least the most talked-about) area for them in terms of our relationships is the emptiness experienced through heart interest in or involvement with the opposite sex. Thus, that inherent relational challenge could well be likened to the ever-restless wind described in the above Scripture.

Men frequently term women heart-on-sleeve creatures. While that's an overstatement and a dismissive simplification, the description nevertheless contains a grain of truth. We women do pack our emotional apparatus close to the surface. Or we might say that as women we tend to consider all our experiences "up close and personal." However we choose to describe feminine emotional wiring, the wiring is thinly insulated—and hence vulnerable. Our vulnerability is particularly evident in male-female relationships.

Within that relational area there are various points at which we women may struggle with feelings of emptiness.

THE EMPTINESS OF SINGLENESS

Whatever her background, part of a woman's created nature yearns for the fulfillment of marriage. Cultural expectations—particularly in Christian circles—also pressure her toward marriage. Hence, the very thought of singleness may loom as a threatening empty place. Some troubling voids expressed to me have included the following:

- Absence of any masculine interest beyond casual friendships
- One or more nonprogressing emotional attachments
- A broken engagement
- A no-show groom on the wedding day
- Divorce
- Widowhood

In dealing with the topic of the single woman, I believe it's important to begin by establishing a solid, sound, and scriptural foundation. Singleness forms a unique world within the general universe of couples and families surrounding it. But misconceptions, misplaced emphases, and careless generalizations have cast a negative shadow over the world of singles.

Let me urge the married woman reading this book not to skip this chapter, or to skim it carelessly, but, please, read thoughtfully—not only to expand your compassionate understanding of single women but also to keep in mind the sobering realization that each of us married women is personally just one heartbeat away from being single!

A STARTING POINT

The single girl or woman herself may need a major attitude adjustment. She needs to examine her mindset carefully and honestly.

When she finds (as almost all will) that she yearns for romance and marriage, that desire must be wholeheartedly submitted to God's will. Actually, of course, such life commitment ought not to be one made only by singles. According to Scripture it should, rather, be part of every believer's whole-soul determination to do God's will in every aspect of life. As individuals we are to kneel as did Jesus Christ in Gethsemane and pray, "Not my will, but thine be done." But for girls and women it's extremely hard to put the desire for marriage on the altar of sacrifice. We want instead to go to the altar (the wedding altar)!

It's a sad fact that Christian circles are permeated with a "coupling fixation" that convinces girls from childhood that marriage is a must. Instead, we parents, teachers, and mentors desperately need to instruct and model the truth for our girls through all their growing-up years that womanly wholeness does not demand romance or marriage. When we teach or infer otherwise, we dangerously contradict a basic tenet of Christianity.

> And ye are complete in him [Christ], which is the head of all principality and power. (Colossians 2:10)

Our unintentional elevation of coupling as a must actually plays into the hands of Satan, who is using that "must" propaganda to destroy lives wholesale.

The unsaved world has so distorted the man-woman relationship that girls are inundated with wrong concepts of every sort. That makes it all the more imperative that as Christians we shape feminine standards, goals, and concept of self according to God's Word. A passage of Scripture that can help us rightly mold our girls is Psalm 144:12*b*—

> That our daughters may be as corner stones, polished after the similitude of a palace.

A cornerstone is—in and of itself—a thing of beauty, strength, and special purpose. Some of the most important cornerstones in the household of faith throughout history and into our present time are single women. Why, then, is singleness so often considered emptiness—particularly for a woman?

Christians often come up with the reflexive "Well, God said it wasn't good for the man to be alone, so . . ." "He created woman to be man's companion, so . . ." Instead of being reflexive (as in knee-jerk), let's reflect deeply upon the subject.

- In Genesis God was talking about a specific man at the time: Adam.
- He created a specific woman—Eve—for that specific man.
- In bringing Eve to Adam God didn't declare a universal "must" or "should."
- The Creator's specific, individualized dealing there in Eden should remind us that He works just as personally with us today.
- Throughout His Word the Lord shows us single women whose completeness, worth, and service are unmistakable.
- The apostle Paul tells us in I Corinthians that marriage can actually minimize effective life ministry.

I say therefore to the unmarried and widows, It is good for them if they abide even as I. (I Corinthians 7:8)

There is a difference also between a wife and a virgin. The unmarried woman careth for the things of the Lord, that she may be holy in body and in spirit: but she that is married careth for the things of the world, how she may please her husband. (I Corinthians 7:34)

I feel strongly about the aspersions cast upon singleness in our Christian circles. We thereby do a great disservice not only to adult women who are unmarried but to the younger generation coming on, as well. It is sad to see how we marginalize single women, fail to minister effectively to them, and fail to encourage them to serve the Lord with their unique capacity to do so. Although our treatment of singles as second-class citizens may be unintentional, it's nonetheless a major failure in caring for all members of the body of Christ.

Marginalizing singles

Single women are set apart in a number of ways. In fact, the term *single* itself can be instructive about the constancy with which we do so. In speaking of acquaintances, for instance, don't we often say, "She's single," as if that were a particular identification? Why? By contrast, we would rarely say, "She's married" about the nonsingle person. Or we use "cute" terms—"She's an unclaimed blessing." Whether subtle or strong, the meaning is clear: a single woman is a misfit. Shame on us! I challenge you, too, to become aware of the vocal tones, inflective innuendos, and outright belittling or dismissive comments used when speaking with or about single women. Those attitudes paint singleness in repulsive colors you'll not find anywhere in God's Word. That wrong portraiture is having disastrous effects. It instills terror in the hearts of high school and college girls; they feel that unless they find a man they'll miss out on life itself. It makes them vulnerable to male predators, and it leads many into ghastly marriage choices.

Why would we misrepresent and mistreat our single sisters? In most cases, it's probably the result of unclear thinking or carryover from attitudes of our predecessors. Sometimes I've also sensed a bit of underlying envious resentment—because singles have a level of independence and freedom denied us married women.

Men's actions and attitudes toward single women are quite easily discernible: they're rooted in the male ego. "After all, what's any
woman without a man?" comes through loud and clear.

A sad fact for us as Christians is that because we wrongly consider single women, we fail to minister adequately to them. Fun-
damental, Bible-preaching churches generally do a poor job of
nurturing that particular part of the flock. Consider how our focus
leaves them on the fringes: sermon emphases, banquet themes, re-
treats, family fellowships, and so forth. Within the general ministry
of a church, singles may be treated as part of the youth group—
forever. Or they're "naturally" put into the ladies' Sunday school
class. But isn't the class taught by a married woman and doesn't
it primarily address marriage and family concerns? We need to
awaken to the fact that singles are the fastest-growing segment of
American society; their ages range from post-high-school to senior
citizens. Why aren't we doing a better job of addressing their needs
and using their gifts?

What about ministry opportunities open to single women? In
many cases they're minimal. There seems to be a general mindset
that a woman is not fit for service if she's unmarried. Truth to tell,
however, just the opposite may be true. I personally know single
women who are light-years beyond their married counterparts spiritually. The apostle Paul clearly saw the contrast between single and
married believers in their service for the Lord. God moved him to
pass that understanding on to us in the passage quoted earlier from
I Corinthians.

And a final consideration of our wrong attitudes: we often unwittingly use and abuse our singles. How? Think about it—single
women are almost always included on guest lists for bridal and baby
showers ("They must have extra money since they don't have a family of their own"). Now wait a minute; we who are married come

to "payback time" with such occasions, don't we? Our daughter gets a bridal shower, or our grandchild is welcomed with a baby shower. The single doesn't ever so benefit—she just gives and gives and gives.

Numberless last-minute pleas for help go out to the singles ("She doesn't have anything to do in the evenings—she could make the banquet decorations . . . or babysit . . . or . . .").

Single schoolteachers are not just loaded with classes and extracurriculars; they're overloaded. The thinking of supervisors and parents seems to be "She's single; she needs these things to keep her busy. Our married folks just don't have the time." These are only a few examples of the regrettable way we treat singles.

Married reader, do you begin to understand how one of your unmarried sisters may carry within her a sense of emptiness? And, single reader, when treatments like the above and similar demonstrations of thoughtlessness come your way, how can you respond properly?

A WOMAN'S HOUSE OF SELF

In order to consider what should or should not mark our responses, we really must begin by analyzing personal essence: what you are will determine what you think, do, and say. So let's zero in on your individual being—whether you've never been married, you're married, you're divorced, or you're a widow. Each of us has the responsibility to build our "house" of self and life. Proverbs 9:1 puts it this way:

> Wisdom hath builded her house, she hath hewn out her seven
> pillars.

A house having seven pillars is a mighty fine residence! It's certainly no shack or carelessly assembled factory prefab. That's you, Christian: an important dwelling place, housing the blessed Holy Spirit. It's speaking of an individual house—not a cluster of homes or a crowded apartment building, and not a place labeled either "married" or "unmarried."

As a believer, our house of self has been specifically designed, constructed, and situated by the Master Architect: He is the living Wisdom of the Ages. That certainly should give assurance of rightness in the construction and placement, shouldn't it?

As a born-again Christian your house is on an eternally sure foundation: the Rock, Jesus Christ. Full confidence can be yours as you face whatever storms life may bring your way. Consider the solidity upon which you stand—not the slippery slope of man's opinions, nor the shifting sands of human emotions, nor the treacherous shale of reasoned evaluation.

> My soul, wait thou only upon God; for my expectation is from
> him. He only is my rock and my salvation: he is my defence; I
> shall not be moved. In God is my salvation and my glory: the
> rock of my strength, and my refuge, is in God. (Psalm 62:5–7)

Seven pillars should span across the facade of the Christian woman's structure: seven tall, straight, beautifying columns "hewn out"—carefully, painstakingly formed to proclaim the dwelling's individuality. I think of them as columns of godly femininity:

CLEANLINESS	CONSTITUTION	CARRIAGE	CHARACTER	CONDITION	CONDUCT	COUNTENANCE
the clean self-giving evidence of a cleansed soul	the bodily evidence of wisely tended health	the upright physical bearing reflecting uprightness of spirit	the key to all the other columns' alignment	the attitudes and emotions that are stable toward humanity and honoring toward God	the behavior illustrating what you claim to believe	a face expressing inward joy and out-flowing love

My dear friend, God will honor, bless, and use a woman with such a house—regardless of her marital state.

My sessions with single women, whatever particular age, area of singleness, or cause for singleness they may represent, have also underlined for me the need to urge the unmarried Christian woman to establish and practice some protective measures.

SPIRITUAL DETERMINATION

In presenting the following, I must give credit to the anonymous student, whoever she was, who long years ago either found or composed the material to follow: "Declaration of Commitment for the Single Girl." She passed it along to a former teacher, who in turn passed it to me. Since then, due to the solidity and excellence of the piece, I have recommended it to generations of my own students.

DECLARATION OF COMMITMENT
FOR THE SINGLE GIRL

God is my heavenly Father. He is the all-wise One Who controls all things. His essence is love and His desire is for my good.

Since He is loving enough to desire only good for me, and wise enough to plan just what is best, and powerful enough to accomplish what His love and goodness have planned, how can I lack any good thing?

It is to this certainty that I make unconditional surrender of all that I am and all that I have. I belong to Him.

Especially do I now present to Him all my normal desires to be married and to have a home and children, realizing He has my best interests in view.

I give to Him my "right" to date and to be married, and purpose to thank Him for whatever He allows to come to me. Especially do I declare that my social life belongs to God, not to me. I yield to Him my desire to date a particular young man or fellows in general. I will take what privileges God might give me to date as opportunities for personal edification and enjoyment, but especially as opportunities for His glory in my attitude and actions.

I purpose to trust God's love, goodness, and wisdom regarding His plan for my future—whether or not it includes marriage. I believe that He will not "withhold any good thing from me" and if He deems it wise to withhold marriage, I trust Him to give grace and glory—grace to keep me from pursuing and/or using my innate desire for anything other than His purposes, and glory that my life may be a happy, fulfilled, and beautiful testimony for Him regardless of my marital state. (Psalm 84:11)

I purpose to refuse any thoughts of self-pity, jealousy, criticism, or resentment which threaten to creep in when I have no man-woman social life, when it seems prayer for it goes unanswered, or when I cannot understand God's way with me now or His intention for my future.

I will refer to and renew this commitment at the following times:

1. Today

2. Daily—for fortification as needed

3. When confronted by doubt or self-pity

MENTAL COMMITMENT

A single woman's control and direction of her thinking will make a huge deposit in or withdrawal from her peace of mind account. Basic to success, of course, is the individual's daily soaking in Scripture. Memorize specific passages addressing your chinks-in-the-armor areas (e.g., self-pity, fear, loneliness). We can think God's thoughts after Him only when we know those thoughts.

While directing attention into the Word, direct it against the world—wherever and however it threatens your chinks in the armor. Just a few examples are romantic music, romance novels and films, bride magazines (and most women's magazines in general!), daytime TV, and nighttime TV.

PHYSICAL COMMITMENT

Physical yearning for caresses, kisses, and sexual fulfillment are a biological fact. They are not, however, necessary to sustain life or to make it fully meaningful. The physical yearnings mentioned are cyclical or wavelike in us women. Some days there will be no problem. But other days yearning may be intense. Mount extra guard for such times. For example, get active: do intense aerobic exercise, take a cold shower, deep-clean your apartment or house. Direct your attention away from your physical self: tackle a new, interesting hobby or study. Undertake a compassion project. By all means avoid a drawing-into-yourself, a sit-down, or a drown-my-yearning-in-food response. Any of those will worsen matters, not make them better.

Now—with the intention of providing some special encouragement for singles—let's move from principles to personification. In God's own picture gallery hangs the portrait of a dear single woman whose house was built by Jehovah, who raised her columns straight and tall, and who enjoyed a unique, rich reward. She's Anna, and she's found in Luke 2:36-38:

> And there was one Anna, a prophetess, the daughter of Phanuel, of the tribe of Aser: she was of a great age, and had lived with a husband seven years from her virginity; and she was a widow of about fourscore and four years, which departed not from the temple, but served God with fastings and prayers night and day.

Take a close look at Anna. A great deal lies behind the deftly sketched outline. You'll see a woman not only worthy of admiration but also worthy of emulation.

Here is a woman widowed only seven years after she married: the sorrow of loss had come to her early. Apparently, too, she was childless. We can easily recognize her situation as she must have felt it: empty.

When Scripture introduces us, Anna is eighty-four years old.

What has filled all those long, empty, lonely years? What has sustained her amid the pity, thoughtlessness, or shunning those around her may have demonstrated? The answer is simple—again, not easy, but simple—she responded with wisdom. God indicates the excellence of her wisdom in the phrase "a prophetess." She was a woman steeped in the things of God. See how godly wisdom played out in her choices.

She wisely chose proper surroundings: she lived in the temple. That infers she turned her attention away from the ordinary concerns of life. She didn't go out looking for sympathy or help from others in her widowhood; she didn't look to see if there were some eligible bachelor or widower who might marry and care for her. By living in the temple she chose protection for her naturally weak human flesh. By living there she garnered the fellowship and encouragement of other godly souls. By living there she encouraged her personal pursuit of holiness.

She wisely chose to respond to life's difficulties with a proper spirit. She hadn't retreated into the temple so that she could enjoy sympathy and service; she was there in dedicated, active service for the Lord. Her spirit of involvement proclaimed wholehearted love for God. Her service was one of privacy and self-denial. She wasn't leading the choir or playing the organ, enjoying the appreciation of such public display. She was fasting and praying—spiritual activities that demand tremendous self-discipline. Her service was unstinting: she didn't go in at 8:00 and get off at 5:00. She didn't have five-day workweeks and then spend weekends at the lake. She served night and day.

Indeed, Anna's was a house of self to which we can each look for challenge, whether we're single or married. God ultimately blessed that wisely built house with a moment so glorious it transcended all she had ever known or hoped for. There, in the midst of her familiar, unglamorous, faithful, unadvertised service she saw the infant Jesus. Though the baby lay in the arms of a common, roughly clad couple, Anna's old eyes recognized Him to be the Christ, her longed-for Messiah. That instant identification really should not strike us as surprising: Anna had focused on God's face throughout all her years there in the temple. No wonder she knew Him!

No matter what experiences may mark her individual situation, the single Christian woman who rightly builds and maintains her house of self, like Anna, can know spiritual strength, godly wisdom, a joyful spirit, and important service for God.

❦ THINKING IT OVER ❦

Does singleness seem a giant empty place? If so, it's because we've created and maintained that daunting Goliath. But remember that although the enormous physical fellow of that name held Israel's army at bay with his roaring, one small individual with one small stone turned human towering timber to fallen log.

We Christian women need to stop our ears to the man-is-essential roar of the Singleness Goliath. His effect on our community of believers is shameful. You and I have at our disposal a mighty stone, the Word of God, which will fell the giant. Like David, we can rightly begin our campaign by saying, "Is there not a cause?" (I Samuel 17:29b).

CHAPTER TWELVE

EMPTINESS
IN MARRIAGE

BETTER IS AN HANDFUL WITH QUIETNESS, THAN BOTH THE
HANDS FULL WITH TRAVAIL AND VEXATION OF SPIRIT.

ECCLESIASTES 4:6

The empty places single women experience are often worse in the
lives of their married sisters.

Once married, a woman's emotional self knows intensified focus
because of her commitment to her husband. As the human axis of
her world, he has unique power to inflict pain. The hurt's severity
of course parallels the seriousness of the relational difficulty. Some
marital empty places expressed to me have included the following:

- Cooled romance
- Clashing temperaments and personalities
- The husband's thoughtless, demanding attitude toward
  his wife
- Inability to please; husbandly criticism or belittling
- The husband's exclusive, isolating immersion in a hobby,
  job, TV, or sports

- The husband's spiritual deadness, shallowness, or hypocrisy
- Emotional, mental, verbal, or physical abuse

Let's walk through those together.

A COOLED SPIRIT OF ROMANCE

This wifely complaint of course points accusingly at her husband: his unsatisfactory attitude and behavior. But let's burrow through externals to the underlying structure playing into the situation. Every husband is a man. By nature a man's romantic inclination is pretty much confined to his wooing period: that time when he's pursuing the woman he wants to marry. He's trying to "make the sale." In that vein, he concentrates on what pleases and magnetizes her. His romantic creative juices flow freely. Once married, however, he reverts to his normal workaday mode. Shakespeare put it accurately and succinctly:

> Man is April when he woos,
> December when he weds.

In view of the universality and normality of the masculine pattern, we women need to recognize that "I need" and "He doesn't . . ." are not the place to begin discussing this marital empty place. Instead, let's start with "Maybe he needs . . ." and "Maybe I don't . . ."

We can picture romance as a delicate flowering plant. It springs up and blooms readily in prenuptial days; in marriage it must be constantly, carefully nurtured. Examine yourself within your marriage relationship. For a wife, cultivating the much-desired romantic bloom basically means inspiring it by her own spirit and example. But how can a wife manage such inspiration amid the daily pressures of living? It has to begin with a brutally honest self-examination of her present spirit and example.

What things do you dislike in your husband, and what is your attitude and behavior toward those things? Before marriage you saw him as perfect (or perfectible). Once married, however, your eyes suddenly beheld his imperfections. If there's impatience, irritation, or disgust toward his flaws, pull yourself to a screeching halt. You are not only killing the seed of romance but you're also jeopardizing your entire marriage relationship. More important, though, you're violating God's clear instruction of Ephesians 5:33—

And the wife see that she reverence her husband.

Lest as you read this you suspect me of trying to instruct from the removed, exalted position of a mere observer or an exemplar of wifely accomplishment, let me assure you that's not the case. I'm standing right here struggling along beside you, friend! According to my *American Heritage Dictionary*, reverence is "a feeling of profound awe and respect and often love; veneration." In other words, it's the highest form of respect. It's to that standard God calls us Christian wives!

Why is it so difficult to obtain and maintain the kind of respect God wants a wife to have for her husband? Because of the unique and constant closeness of the marriage relationship. Nothing escapes the gaze, and much can prove abrasive simply by walking so closely with one another day by day.

There is an observable journey to a woman's marital disenchantment. Where exists the wife who has not witnessed a major dual transformation: her husband from knight in shining armor to man in laundered underwear. In other words, who has not plummeted from heights of expected ecstasy to the valley of actual experience? Though unsettling, the plunge must be made in order for genuine, sweeter love to take root: mature love is not an airborne plant. Let's examine the *from* and *to* phrases used above to describe the transformations of man and woman after they marry.

From knight to man. Knights ceased to exist long ago, and they must have been pretty unpleasant to live with, considering all that scratchy armor and the smell of their sweat plus that of their horses. Man, however, continues to exist: male, greatly differing from female.

From shining armor to laundered underwear. Armor was made by a metalworker. Full body armor hid the wearer, making him appear heroic and invincible. Underwear is laundered by a fellow's wife. It reveals him as human and vulnerable.

Then there's our own transformation to consider. In the freshness of courtship we're a maiden in awe—someone influenced by romantic haze to a near-worshipful state of mind. Marriage clears the haze and transforms maiden-in-awe to maid-in-argh—she who's a practical, experienced caretaker. *Argh* is a wordless vocal expression reflecting the inevitable maiden-to-maid journey. A joke my husband tells occasionally summarizes the concept:

Question: Why does a bride wear white?
Answer: To coordinate with the household appliances.

Argh! The emotional meaning with which the sound is uttered reveals the wife's spirit and prophesies much about the ongoing marriage relationship. It can say disappointment, self-pity, disgust, ridicule, or amusement in shared humanity and experience. The latter, of course, is not only preferred but essential.

The bride is not the only half of the couple making a difficult transition. Just as she must adjust her view of and responses to the splendid bridegroom-become-burping-husband, so he must survive the radiant-bride-to-snoring-wife transformation. Marriage, in short, wholly exposes personal verities and vulnerabilities.

There he stands—your man in laundered underwear. What does he need? Many things, with all of them reflecting his man-ness. I've come to believe (belatedly!) that a Christian wife's real success lies in obeying that brief instructional phrase from Scripture quoted earlier:

> And the wife, see that she reverence her husband.

Look closely at the phrase. *Reverence* is used as a verb. It's an action word: you and I are to actively live it out. Frankly, that's a tough assignment. I'm going to head you into that assignment by simply listing the words and phrases inherent in the word *reverence* (from *The Amplified Bible*).

- Notices him
- Regards him
- Honors him
- Prefers him
- Venerates and esteems him
- Defers to him
- Praises him
- Loves and admires him exceedingly

Do you see why I wouldn't dare presume to write as one who has obtained? In fact, I doubt that any mortal woman could honestly do so! And at this point, awareness may strike, bringing us to the second consideration posed at the beginning of this chapter: "Maybe I don't . . ." Whenever or wherever our don'ts show up, they can be romance quenchers in our men.

Why would a wife's lack of esteem for her husband quench his ardor? Because respect is his core need in marriage. I think we women poorly understand that a man feels neither secure nor loved apart from being respected.

My forever-picture-making brain sees me as putting my husband either on a pedestal or on a bed of nails from day to day as I demonstrate respect or disrespect for him. And living out reverence's defining phrases doesn't mean I have to be moon-eyed, syrupy, or sappy. Rather, I can express each one in ways that accord with my temperament and personality, his, and the unique personality of our relationship itself.

Interestingly, a husband will not only appreciate his wife's genuine display of respect; he'll also interpret it as romantic and be encouraged toward romance in return.

To transition between the normal, unavoidable romance-to-reality marriage challenge and more serious problems, we'll turn to another of Solomon's observations.

> Two are better than one; because they have a good reward for their labour. For if they fall, the one will lift up his fellow: but woe to him that is alone when he falleth; for he hath not another to help him up. Again, if two lie together then they have heat: but how can one be warm alone? And if one prevail against him, two shall withstand him; and a threefold cord is not quickly broken. (Ecclesiastes 4:9–12)

Applying the "two are better than one" to marriage, the passage presents a number of interesting thoughts. The specific point to weigh in here is the mention of a threefold cord. Following the positives about two-ness, the triple strand remark may seem to be a disconnect. Instead, it can stand as the highlight of the section: the effective, consistent operation of duos is enabled, protected, and made durable through the addition of a third entity. That principle powerfully applies to the marriage relationship as God comes actively into the equation. Without Him, pressures and strains can quickly break the marriage cord.

We need now to tackle situations experienced in marriage that present challenges going beyond—in some instances far beyond—cooled romance.

CLASHING TEMPERAMENTS AND PERSONALITIES

This is not at all unusual. In fact, though *clashing* may be too strong a term to describe most couples, every combination of personalities and temperaments poses challenge.

The old saying "Opposites attract" generally holds true. Our basic structure is drawn to someone of an unlike type: timid to outgoing or quiet to lugubrious, for example. Much of the attraction harks back to our perceived empty places. That is, sensing or imagining our deficiency in some area, we're drawn to an apparent source of filling or compensation. (At the same time, of course, prospective life mates also look for and value areas of sameness—as in general life purpose and personal interests.) The unique relationship of marriage puts even the smallest differences under a magnifying glass: the resulting distortion can be deadly.

Candlelight, flowers, formal attire, and an organ playing wedding music predispose a couple to picture their life together in tones of pink perfection. Perfection's pink wilts faster than the wedding flowers, and reality's light makes personal differences glaringly evident. If husband and wife, instead of working to mesh in areas of difference, substitute mashing, trouble and pain result. By mashing I mean attempting to force the other person into a preconceived mold or to mash and thus destroy opposing characteristics. In either case, being the mashee is agonizing.

Let's first admit a tough truth: we women are bent toward restructuring. Therefore, the preponderance of nonmeshing problems may be ours. If you're a wife who somehow has tried or is now trying to reshape your husband in any way, I'd say as loudly and clearly as possible, QUIT! But, looking back to the preceding sentence, isolate its opening word, *if*, and let it percolate a moment on your mental and emotional front burner. You may have carried on a reshape campaign without realizing it. For instance, you may have focused disapproving attention upon some habit, characteristic, or behavior that you feel limits him socially or professionally. Female fix-it tendencies, however, are not friends to marital unity. So put away whatever tools you've been using. Let the poor fellow out of the vise and off the workbench. Chisels, vises, and workbenches not only discourage romance but they also damage love.

Maybe, though, your marriage is one in which you're in the vise, and your husband is wielding hammer and chisel. Ouch! I've been there. My husband shares with men—individually and when addressing groups—how determinedly he tried to reshape me. He is strong, managerial, and a talker; I am timid, compliant, and a nontalker. For years Bob made it plain that my structure was flawed, and he worked to reshape me into his image. The harder he worked at it, the more I shrank in the very areas he sought to expand. Finally, pain drove me to state my case: I appealed to him to let me off the workbench. He not only did so but also realized that he had been hammering and chiseling away at the very things that had initially drawn him to me and that they were qualities contributing to the wholeness and balance of our marriage.

So if you're on the receiving end of reshape work, take heart. Of course you're not perfect. But the characteristics of your temperament and personality are components that contribute not only to your unique individuality but also to the wholeness of your marriage. Ask the Lord to show you where you really should change and do so. In those areas where your simple "you-ness" is under attack, seek God's direction, control, timing, and expressive ability; then appeal to your husband, asking him to allow you to be yourself.

Reworking belongs in a factory setting; acceptance and appreciation are homegrown plant food for love. Personality or temperament differences can be either delightful or destructive in marriage. The partners themselves make the choice.

Masculine Poverty of
Thoughtfulness but Wealth of Demands

A Christian woman generally goes into marriage recognizing and desiring her helper-role assignment. But she also has a legitimate expectation that her husband's love will make him considerate and appreciative of her in that role. Unfortunately the masculine "December" postmarital tendency mentioned earlier can become a thoughtless "management" mindset.

I'll begin this section by urging each of us wives to examine the scale on which we weigh our husband's thoughtfulness. If we mark our scale according to any of the following, the poor man is doomed to shortfall.

- Our father's sweetness toward our mother
- Imagination/expectation of our man's husbandly perfection
- A gentle-souled husband of some friend or acquaintance

We also need to check our hand on the scale: do we give our husband credit and express appreciation for whatever thoughtfulness weight he does register?

There are, of course, husbands whose spirit and behavior in terms of thoughtfulness register zero. In addressing this point my mind turns with immense gratitude to a godly woman who shines as an example of right response to such a husband. Almost immediately after she married, my friend realized she had a tiger by the tail. Her husband is a strong, decisive man of tremendous energy and stamina. After saying "I do," he jumped back into his full schedule, adding several new projects. He scarcely cast a glance toward his wife beyond the demand that she keep up with him and take care to provide all the "etceteras" lending to his comfort and efficiency. At first she felt like you or I would—she resented the callous treatment and was defeated by her undeserved suffering. She came near to chucking the whole marriage. Convicted of the sinfulness in that reaction, she decided instead to become a wife who obeyed Scripture and pleased God. In fact, she determined to redirect the intense emotional desire that was worsening her misery. She made a pact with herself: it didn't matter if she never got a single word of appreciation from her husband; she didn't even want one. She was going to live so that when she got to heaven Jesus Christ Himself would say, "You were a wonderful wife to your husband." Years passed and that dear woman stuck to her resolve. She dedicatedly respected and ministered to her husband's racehorse self and enriched his racetrack life. Then one day she burst into tears: her husband told her she was the most wonderful wife a man could have! She wept in disappointment—because she so earnestly yearned to hear that commendation first from her Savior!

Ideally, of course, wifing is a ministry in which the husband recognizes and commends the service rendered. But when husbandly thoughtfulness and appreciation are missing, they need not create emptiness for the Christian wife. If she goes to the Bible to listen to and learn from the Lover of her soul, she will find consistent strength for her earthly relationship and compensating sweetness in her heavenly relationship.

INABILITY TO PLEASE

Negative, harsh words from one's husband must be a woman's most painfully experienced realization of Proverbs 12:18:

> There is that speaketh like the piercings of a sword.

Such intense, words-induced pain can make a wife curl protectively into herself or lash back with verbal claw and fang. Harsh speech is antithetical to the demands God makes of a husband: it is light-years from the sacrificial, Christlike love he's told to demonstrate. Light-years—that's also how far removed humanity is from divinity. Every wife would revel in husbandly love that reflects divinity; what we get, however—in both of us—is humanity and its many uglies. Demeaning speech is one of those uglies. The three-strand cord principle must remind us that husband and wife are personally responsible before God. Therefore, as a wife I must give over both my husband and the hurt he causes me into the Lord's almighty hands. At the same time, empowered by the Holy Spirit, I am to carry out my own spiritual responsibility. That involves a number of things:

- Accessing God's strength
  Strengthened with all might, according to his glorious power, unto all patience and longsuffering with joyfulness. (Colossians 1:11)

- Avoiding retaliatory speech
  A soft answer turneth away wrath: but grievous words stir up anger. (Proverbs 15:1)

- Activating godly love
  [Love] suffereth long, and is kind. (I Corinthians 13:4)

- Affirming security in Christ and His ultimate reward
  Who will render to every man according to his deeds: to them who by patient continuance in well doing seek for glory and honour and immortality, eternal life. (Romans 2:6–7)

On the human level, you may be living with a husband who is impossible to please. That doesn't excuse you from trying to do so in every legitimate, God-honoring way possible. Moreover, his refusal to be pleased can be the impetus for your transformed focus (as in the case of my friend): from primarily desiring your mate's approval to wholeheartedly desiring to please God.

THE HUSBAND'S EXCLUSIVE, ISOLATING IMMERSION IN A HOBBY, JOB, TV, OR SPORTS

While the words "exclusive, isolating" probably don't apply in most of our marriages, "immersion" almost surely does with regard to something our husband enjoys. Intensity of involvement in a narrow range of interests seems to be a male characteristic; there is a near-compulsive quality to the attention and time men spend pursuing their interests. My husband's pet interests are weather and airplanes. The first makes him addicted to the Weather Channel; the second draws him to pore endlessly over multiple aviation magazines. Although the fascination of those things eludes me, and though it sometimes discourages communication, I've come to accept his interests, recognize them as innocent, and stop resenting his enjoyment of and relaxation in them.

There are men, however, who go overboard in their extracurricular involvements; all of their free time is dedicated to them. That leaves a wife feeling abandoned. It threatens the strength of the marriage bond, leaving her to deal with a deep, aching emptiness. Raging or nagging will have little or no effect, except to drive the husband deeper into his involvement for the sake of protection from the wife's assault.

One young wife stands out in my memory as a wonderful example of creativity and wisdom. She told me how totally absorbed her husband is in auto mechanics. Except to eat and sleep, he spends all of his spare time in the garage behind their home, working on cars and trucks for the sheer fun of it. Realizing early on that griping or shaming tactics didn't work, this dear wife went out, bought herself one of those little wheeled mechanics boards, and began joining her husband under whatever vehicle he happened to be working on! She achieved both communication and togetherness with her mechaniholic.

One workable principle here, simply put, is "If you can't lick 'em, join 'em." A good marriage demands togetherness. When extracurricular interests are seriously working against that vital ingredient, the wise wife's response may be to join her man in his interest. This response, though, must be carefully weighed against an opposing need: private time and involvement for both husband and wife. A living, thriving relationship not only needs plenty of togetherness but also demands breathing space for its individual components.

The Husband's Spiritual Deadness, Shallowness, or Hypocrisy

The empty place experienced by a Christian wife in this situation is broad and deep indeed. Unity of husband and wife is far more than just physical. God intends that there be oneness of mind and spirit, as well. Separation at that core level negatively affects every area of life. Too, a wife clearly recognizes this particular empty place to be utterly beyond her ability to rectify. That very fact, however, can be a strong positive, keeping her from attempting the human solutions she might choose in other types of difficulty.

Though she yearns for her husband's salvation and spiritual growth, a wife must not step in to "help" the Holy Spirit by berating, nagging, or sermonizing. Instead, she needs to mount a prayer campaign asking God to do His desired work in her husband's heart—and in her own. The greater the man's distance from God, the more urgent it is that the wife live God before him. But what a monumental challenge!

> Likewise, ye wives, be in subjection to your own husbands; that,
> if any obey not the word, they also may without the word be won
> by the conversation [manner of life] of the wives. (I Peter 3:1)

Over the past several years I've been in contact with a dear young woman who has exemplified godly living with an ungodly man. Although she'd been saved in her early teens, she married while in a spiritually dangerous state—bitter unforgiveness for her childhood sexual abuse and rebellion against God for having allowed it. Once married, however, she soon awoke to the fact that she had immeasurably worsened her life pain by taking on the unequal yoke of marriage to an unsaved man. God further convicted her for her personal sinful practices, and she gave them up. But her doing so enraged her husband; he wanted her to continue the lifestyle they had shared. Conflict became a daily reality. As children came into the home, she realized her increased responsibility to represent God before them. She clung to I Corinthians 7:13–14—

> And the woman which hath an husband that believeth not,
> and if he be pleased to dwell with her, let her not leave him.
> For the unbelieving husband is sanctified by the wife, and the
> unbelieving wife is sanctified by the husband: else were your
> children unclean; but now are they holy.

Living out that Scripture demanded daily sacrifice of self and constant dependence on the Lord. Though her husband continued with his drinking and partying, she honored him as head of their home. Though he deliberately antagonized her, mocked her desire for church attendance and Christian fellowship, she loved and obeyed him. The way has been long for this woman, and her husband is still unsaved. But God has honored her dedicated life: her children are born again, her husband allows their church attendance, and he now not only treats her adoringly but is also en-

couraging her to have a ministry to other women! I wait eagerly to
hear of his salvation.

In such home-bound battles between righteousness and
unrighteousness, light and dark, the woman of light experiences
constant pressures, opposition, and discouragements of every sort.
Nor is a happy ending guaranteed. Yet the emptiness she experiences in her marriage, that unique and closest of human relationships, can open before her the reality of fullness the prophet Isaiah
expressed long ago:

> Behold, God is my salvation; I will trust, and not be afraid: for
> the Lord Jehovah is my strength and my song; he also is become
> my salvation (Isaiah 12:2).

Notice the bookends of God's salvation in that passage. What
a powerful reminder of its ALL-ness in our lives. The marvelous
sufficiency of salvation assures us of sufficiency from God in every
other area of need, as well.

> He that spared not his own Son, but delivered him up for us
> all, how shall he not with him also freely give us all things?
> (Romans 8:32)

EMOTIONAL, MENTAL, VERBAL, OR PHYSICAL ABUSE

We would like to think such things could never take place in any
marriage. But they do. Herein is sin's dark ugliness indeed. And
yet it is rampant—not just among the unsaved but within our
Christian circles as well. In the latter case, the ugliness is worse,
the blackness deeper because the abuser not only knowingly violates
Scripture but often twists Scripture to justify his behavior. Added
sadness comes through the fact that too many times a husband's
abusiveness is disbelieved, downplayed, ignored, or covered up by
spiritual authorities.

God puts into one particular verse a really startling command for married men:

> Husbands, love your wives, even as Christ also loved the church, and gave himself for it (Ephesians 5:25).

Some men claiming to be Christians turn a bleary or blind eye to that passage while magnifying passages that speak of the husband's headship and wife's submission. They then point to the wife's failures, claiming they give him reason for harshness. How wholly unlike Christ's love for the church!

While every wife, inevitably, will fail at some point, no one deserves a husband's cruelty. And, while every husband at some point will speak or do hurtful things to his wife, no one has the right to follow a pattern of treatment that defies God's Word. A man who batters his wife with words or fists is a bully who must be resisted. There is neither excuse for such unconscionable behavior, nor any excuse for allowing it.

A bully is a coward in disguise. Ineffective with his equals, such a man takes out his anger and frustration on those who are weaker than he. A heartbreaking fact of life within our circles is that a husband's bullying is often excused and justified in the name of wifely submission. That flimsy claim made by a wife batterer, unbelievably, may be accepted by a pastor or other spiritual authority; in some cases, not only is the man excused and the wife chided but the batterer is allowed to continue in a position of service or even as a church officer.

There are numberless scenarios within the category of abuse, and the circumstances and relational factors involved in each case must be taken into consideration. At base, however, is the indisputable fact that an abusive husband is disobeying both God's law and man's law.

The wife therefore has right on her side when she refuses to allow the mistreatment. That refusal can take many forms, and the wife must think carefully and pray earnestly for God's guidance in choosing her specific response. The optimal juncture for standing up against mistreatment is the very first time it happens.

Sometimes a simple word expressing self-respect and refusal to allow ill treatment will put the bully to flight. I saw that happen at close hand. A woman I knew well was a gentle, happy soul; her husband came from an abusive preacher's home. A nonfavorite with his father and unpopular in school, he began early after marriage to prove his manhood and superiority by a dismissive attitude, small cruelties, and harsh words. For too many long years the wife endured it all. Finally, health problems sent her to a medical doctor who had wisdom in matters not physical: he questioned the woman about her marriage relationship. His ultimate prescription was "You have to stand up to your husband. Don't let him continue treating you this way." God made that moment a turning point. The next time the husband began one of his demeaning tirades, his wife quietly but firmly told him she would no longer allow him to talk to her that way. The man certainly did not become an angel. He did, however, greatly improve in his treatment of his wife. The principle of this true story is simple: a bully mistreats someone who allows the mistreatment.

I know of another woman whose husband revealed his brutish nature shortly after their wedding. He verbally battered away at her shaky self-perception, calling her names fit only for addressing dogs. He used money as a leash, allowing her barely enough for household expenses. After children were born to the couple, he delighted in berating her in front of them. For twenty-five years she endured, sustained by her personal faith and Christian fellowship at her church. Finally, when her husband began bringing prostitutes into their home, she called a halt to the miserable situation. Helped by Christian friends, she and the children fled while the bully was away from the house. Since that time, it has been instructive and a blessing to see God's special undertaking for her. He enabled her to win child support, led her to employment that allowed time for her to be both mother and father to her children, and gave her the joy of seeing her children grown to godly adulthood, happily married and producing sweet grandchildren. How tenderly God responds to His truly needy ones!

On the sad side of such situations is a story far different. After one of my sessions with women, an obviously distressed young woman lingered until she could talk with me privately. With horror I listened to her tale of worsening beatings by her husband. She and he were members of a local church, so one day shortly after our talk I accompanied her to the pastor's office. I don't know when I've ever been more disappointed and angry. The girl tried to tell her story—tried—because the pastor only half listened and soon jumped in to talk of a personal experience that had no bearing upon the situation. He ended the conference with a vague indication that he would look into the matter. Whatever the "look" did, it certainly didn't help. In essence, the wife's appeal was dismissed, and her husband was allowed to continue acting the good guy in his area of church service. All too soon I learned of the wife's further dilemma. In our initial meeting, she had told me, with fear, that her husband wanted to move the family far out of town. I warned her against it—isolation is a batterer's key tool. But fear (and failure of the pastor to help) kept her in chains of "submission." Years passed, then not long ago I happened upon this dear woman in a nearby clothing store. I had to look at her repeatedly to assure myself it was she. What I saw and sensed as I spoke to her still brings tears to my eyes. All beauty and sparkle were gone. She was a craven, downtrodden creature. Her voice was the strangest I've ever heard. There was no trace of the normal speech she'd had earlier. What came to my ears could only be called inverted vocal production: she spoke on her inhalations rather than—as is normal—on exhalation. Every word she uttered was, at it were, a gasp of fear, pain, and repression. Although that wretched husband will one day answer at the judgment, years of unnecessary suffering have rolled away. The fault lies in several directions:

- With the wife herself
- With the pastor
- With family and friends who failed to help her

And beyond her own battering looms the awful specter of the children growing to twisted, misshapen adulthood.

Beyond the above three personally known cases of abuse, I've also had many others revealed to me by telephone and mail. In these domestic settings of sadness, there certainly is no paint-by-number recommendation for response. We can, however, be sure of this: God is grieved by such awful, befouled pictures of Christ and His bride, the church! And when the abused woman appeals to Him, He will give the courage and wisdom to respond properly. That response may be revelation of the truth somewhat like Abigail's when she said very honestly to David that her churlish husband Nabal was a "man of Belial . . . Nabal is his name, and folly is with him." Or it may have to be a self-preserving response similar to the young David's long flight from King Saul. Resistance or disclosure or escape—a husband's treatment that must be met with any of those is a living nightmare. The emptiness known by the wife in such a situation is vast indeed. An appropriate prayer for her lips is that found in Psalm 64:1–6—

> Hear my voice, O God, in my prayer: preserve my life from fear
> of the enemy. Hide me from the secret counsel of the wicked;
> from the insurrection of the workers of iniquity: who whet their
> tongue like a sword, and bend their bows to shoot their arrows,
> even bitter words; that they may shoot in secret at the perfect:
> suddenly do they shoot at him, and fear not. They encourage
> themselves in an evil matter: they commune of laying snares
> privily; they say, Who shall see them? They search out iniquities:
> they accomplish a diligent search: both the inward thought of
> every one of them, and the heart, is deep.

The marriage relationship abounds with challenges; it is impossible for husband and wife to relate to one another perfectly. But every relational imperfection can know improvement as we surrender the situation, the other person(s), and ourselves to the Lord. Our puzzlement will give way to comprehension as we diligently search the Word. Our relational incapabilities will be exchanged for His enabling as we petition His power.

THINKING IT OVER

The apostle Paul's first letter to Thessalonian believers ends with the benediction,

> And the very God of peace sanctify you wholly; and I pray God
> your whole spirit and soul and body be preserved blameless unto
> the coming of our Lord Jesus Christ (I Thessalonians 5:23).

Notice the emphasis on wholeness in the passage. God's desire is that our preservation be fully effective, infusing all of our being, spirit and soul and body—and all of our life—unto the coming of our Lord Jesus Christ.

Isn't it interesting that the opening focus upon our self in the verse is the spirit—the motivating, pervading, aura-producing entity within each of us. It's the spirit in us that seems to yield most readily to Satan's pickling efforts. Our spirit can suffer and sour if we respond wrongly to our relational empty places. Consider, for example, your own circle of Christian friends and acquaintances. All may have lips that witness of their salvation, activities and appearance that indicate protective monitoring of their bodies. Ah, but what of their spirit? Matters aren't nearly so positive in that regard, are they? Most any group of Christian women today is worried and weakened by the nonpeaceful, unsanctified spirit of its members as they

- Complain—belittle
- Criticize—snipe
- Whine—betray
- Accuse—malign
- Resent—undercut
- Gossip—compete

Those and other negatives of spirit mar us individually, mangle interpersonal relationships, and marginalize personal testimony. If brought to account for such unbecoming realities, the explanation or justification may be something like the following: "Well, you see the truth of the matter is, I've never had . . . I need . . . I wasn't taught . . ." In other words, "If it weren't for my empty place(s), I could be what I should be."

No, rather, we can be what we should be if we recognize our empty places, individually and interpersonally, to be opportunities for God's filling.

As that full-to-the-brim apostle, Paul, prayed for Ephesian believers, so I close our contemplations together in this chapter:

> That the God of our Lord Jesus Christ, the Father of glory, may give unto you the spirit of wisdom and revelation in the knowledge of him: the eyes of your understanding being enlightened; that ye may know what is the hope of his calling,

and what the riches of the glory of his inheritance in the saints, and what the exceeding greatness of his power to us-ward who believe . . . the fullness of him that filleth all in all (Ephesians 1:17–19, 23).

CHAPTER THIRTEEN

No Empty Places

LET US HEAR THE CONCLUSION OF THE WHOLE MATTER:
FEAR GOD, AND KEEP HIS COMMANDMENTS: FOR THIS IS THE
WHOLE DUTY OF MAN. FOR GOD SHALL BRING EVERY WORK
INTO JUDGMENT, WITH EVERY SECRET THING, WHETHER IT BE
GOOD, OR WHETHER IT BE EVIL.

ECCLESIASTES 12:13-14

No matter who she is, where she lives, or what she does by way
of profession, a woman at some point recognizes and responds to
empty places: they are part and parcel of her earthly existence—
but they are not always negatives. For the unsaved person, the
emptiness may be the first thing to awaken a need for God's filling through salvation. For the born-again Christian, hollowness
should recall us to closer fellowship with and greater dependence
upon Jesus Christ.

But can the concept of Christ's fullness be translated into what
Scripture calls our "conversation"—our daily living? Absolutely.

God Himself gives us a flesh-and-blood example of a woman who responded to her empty places so well that He calls her great. She's the woman of II Kings 4—the Shunammite. This dear woman for years has given me measureless personal blessing. Whereas Proverbs 31 presents an exhausting list of desirable feminine characteristics, the woman of Shunem is a flesh-and-blood demonstration that they really are attainable.

No matter how many times you may have read the passage, I hope you'll open your Bible now, and let's mine each verse for the spiritual wealth it contains. The veins run deep and the ore is rich.

We don't know her name or her specific age. There's nothing told us of her physical appearance—height, weight, coloring, and so forth. We learn nothing of her past.

The Shunammite just appears—all at once and anonymously—as a full-grown adult. The absence of those facts reminds me how unimportant such things are in the eternal sense. Rather, as in the case of the Shunammite, our inner self as revealed in attitudes, words, and actions should be our focus—because, obviously, it is God's focus.

Going through the passage, I'll highlight specific veins of gold; I'd ask you to stop at each one, look searchingly at that particular aspect of the Shunammite, then quiet your heart and ask the Lord to personalize, to use that shining vein for the enrichment of your soul and the spiritual enhancement of your life. While I'm going to point out a few of the things that so convict me personally, you'll doubtless find others for yourself as you study this amazing woman.

> And it fell on a day, that Elisha passed to Shunem, where was a great woman; and she constrained him to eat bread. And so it was, that as oft as he passed by, he turned in thither to eat bread. (II Kings 4:8)

This verse introduces us to our exemplary woman, and it sets the stage for all that follows. The little phrase "on a day" refers to a time frame and turns our attention to the historical setting. That day was a difficult one; this woman's life of faith was not lived out in a setting of political and cultural ease any more than yours and mine are. Other passages reveal that Ahab and then his son Jehoram were on the throne of Israel. The very name Ahab rings with tones of wickedness, and Jehoram followed in his father's footsteps. Evil in leadership contributes to evil in the population at large. Essentially, then, we see a woman who exemplifies godly living in an ungodly time. How appropriate for you and me! We live in a day when America is giving ever-clearer evidence of past evil in high places and spreading evil throughout government and society. Nevertheless, each of us who knows God is responsible to "live godly in Christ Jesus" rather than whining about and excusing ourselves because of dark times and wicked people.

"Elisha passed to Shunem." Elisha was Elijah's replacement as God's outstanding prophet of the day, a man of great faith who was powerfully used by Jehovah. Shunem, a village in the territory of Issachar, near Mount Gilboa, was an unremarkable place. But there in a common place a woman demonstrated an uncommon life of faith.

How interesting it is to consider her evaluation: "where was a great woman." It was made by God Himself and recorded in His Word. Yet had you or I lived in Shunem with this woman, even as next-door neighbors, the term *great* probably would not have occurred to us. As following verses show, she was simply a housewife. Some translations use the term *wealthy* or *rich* instead of *great*. However, she doesn't appear to have had material abundance as we move on through the story. Certainly, though, the narrative reveals that whatever her material possessions, in spiritual terms she most certainly was a *great* woman. The ordinary was made extraordinary by God's grace.

"And she constrained him to eat bread"—this phrase tells us the woman was not bound up in her own concerns; she reached out with active compassion to the itinerate preacher. She "constrained him"; he wasn't asking for her help—she recognized his need and responded to it. Yet, think how demanding her daily housewifery was—she lacked electricity, piped-in water, washer, dryer, dishwasher, refrigerator, microwave, and other modern items. Her compassionate heart made her volunteer extra work for her hands.

"And so it was, that as oft as he passed by, he turned in thither to eat bread." Her care of the prophet was not just a single incident; it became a regular occurrence. And apparently Elisha's travels took him by her house frequently. One act of kindness is not unusual, but extending hospitality unnumbered times says something important about the Shunammite. She ungrudgingly recognized, accepted, and carried a ministry burden. But, you may ask, "Why use the word *ministry?*" Because that's exactly what the Shunammite did for Elisha: she ministered to his physical needs. Obviously she's worthy of our attention.

"And she said to her husband, Behold now, I perceive that this is an holy man of God, which passeth by us continually." We've noted the historical period; we've had the general setting presented; we've had a brief introduction to the characters and situation. Now God opens the door of the Shunammite's home, and we get our first glimpse inside.

To this point all has been merely a landscape painted with a broad brush of narrative. No more. The broad brush is laid aside, and the detailing begins—detailing that will ultimately provide a portrait of a flesh-and-blood woman. Her humanity draws us to identify with her, and her godly heart transcending that humanity can inspire us. Look closely: "She said unto her husband." The remainder of the story makes it unmistakably clear that this woman, rather than her husband, was the spiritual one in the household. The husband never said or did anything indicative of a soul that seeks after Jehovah—he was a spiritual zero. So the Shunammite's household had a huge empty place. While the husband saw only a traveler, her God-ward heart recognized Elisha as a valid prophet. But she did not allow her husband's lack of spiritual interest to stifle hers, or to make her withdraw into self-pity and complaint. Rather, into the human vacuum she invited the divine fullness—she exercised her individual relationship with Jehovah.

In case a single woman reading this book wonders how these particular details can apply to her, just substitute the term *authority* for *husband* as we look more and more into the Shunammite's response to and treatment of him. The principles of her spirit, behavior, and words can certainly apply to employment or ministry relationships.

So let's examine this first indication of her at-home, everyday godliness: "She said unto her husband." The spirit she evidenced here is noteworthy. She made a simple, direct statement (once—no nagging!). She didn't take it upon herself to act apart from her husband. She didn't berate him for his spiritual shortfall. She didn't talk condescendingly to him. She didn't preach him a sermon or shame him for his lack of spiritual stature. By God's grace she experienced sweet spiritual fullness despite the emptiness of her husband's spiritual self. What a powerful example of godly wifing the Shunammite sets for Christian women whose husbands are less than they should be spiritually! She lived out I Peter 3:1 centuries before God moved the apostle to write it.

But go on; look at the remark she makes to her husband: "I perceive that this is an holy man of God that passeth by us continually."

The Shunammite possessed and exercised discernment. But how? What is discernment? The answer is inherent in the word she used: *perceive*. Perception does not come from reason, logic, or emotion, although all three of those may be involved. The perception this woman demonstrated comes as an endowment of wisdom from Jehovah. Her perception operated quietly and surely—she didn't dither. She didn't stew in indecision. Because she accessed wisdom from above, she was guided, guarded, and rewarded. The same results come to you and me as we seek the mind of God and act according to His leading.

Evidently the road leading past the Shunammite's front door was much traveled. She recognized a true prophet of God walking that road—perhaps from among many others. Notice that she did not make her evaluation hastily; she observed Elisha over a period of time, as indicated by the words "that passeth by us continually." As the prophet repeatedly visited their home, she observed him at close range: coming in from various experiences, entering the house after coming through different types of weather, relaxing in the nonpublic setting of her own four walls. She listened to his conversation. She saw his table manners. She saw him express varying moods. She saw him when he was tired at bedtime and when he greeted the day upon arising. Through visit after visit she watched and listened. Then she shared her conclusion with her husband: "This is an holy man of God." She personally differentiated between the true and the false. How could she do so—this ordinary, uneducated housewife? By exercising a simple principle: examine everyone and everything in the light of Truth.

One summer while I was in college I worked in a bank. I opened new accounts and let people into the vault to access their safety deposit boxes. One important part of my training focused on recognizing counterfeit money. I was never shown a phony bill;

instead, I had to do a minute study of genuine US currency. By knowing the true, I would be able to recognize the false. How powerfully that principle should be applied to our daily spiritual life! Only as we consistently study God's truth can we recognize error. Satan is a master at disguising falsehood. He makes his lies sound so convincing and his prophets look so good! Sadly, far too many of today's American Christian women are swept into all sorts of spiritual error, weakening practices, debilitating associations, and harmful influences because they're walking apart from the light of the truth. Sunday-only Scripture isn't sufficient for weekday challenges and trials.

Notice, too, that the woman of Shunem invited only the true prophet into her home. However many others regularly passed her house, however impressive their appearance, whatever feel-good messages they proclaimed, her door was closed to them. The inference and expanded application of that decision can enormously profit Christian homes today. Instead of discerning between truth and error and rejecting the false, believers in America tolerate every shade of falsehood and blithely invite error into their houses. Christian homes are stuffed wall-to-wall with false heroes, false values, false goals. The multiplying, tragic effects of such darkness in our homes are evident everywhere.

Another fact of the Shunammite's recognition of and response to truth skewers me each time I read the passage: the comparative access she had to truth and what you and I have today. Second Kings covers long-ago years in Israel's history, doesn't it? While Jehovah was actively engaged with His people, little of His truth had been put into written form. She couldn't just walk across the room, pick up a Bible, and sit down to study the Old and New Testaments. It would have been rare indeed for such a woman to possess even the merest scrap of Holy Writ. It's evident, however, that she was guided and guarded by the ever-living Word. Her story dramatically highlights God's oft-reiterated promise that those who seek His wisdom will be given that wisdom.

You and I have daily access to the Bible—both Old and New Testaments—the written conduit for God's mind and heart communication with us. That dear Book, however, may seldom if ever be opened between Sundays. Monday through Saturday we tend to operate according to our own inclinations, don't we? So at times of needed discernment we ignore (forget? overlook?) clear warnings against accepting falsehood.

> To the law and to the testimony: if they speak not according to this word, it is because there is no light in them. (Isaiah 8:20)

> Beloved, believe not every spirit, but try the spirits, whether they are of God: because many false prophets are gone out into the world. (I John 4:1)

> If there come any unto you, and bring not this doctrine, receive him not into your house, neither bid him God speed: for he that biddeth him God speed is partaker of his evil deeds. (II John 10–11)

Lessons abound already just within the introductory verse of the passage, don't they? But we'll move on.

> Let us make a little chamber, I pray thee, on the wall; and let us set for him there a bed, and a table, and a stool, and a candlestick: and it shall be, when he cometh to us, that he shall turn in thither. (II Kings 4:10)

The first thing that jumps out at me here is the spirit of the woman's request. Remember, this husband was a spiritual midget. But she didn't take over in the situation: although he lacked soul life and depth, she nevertheless gave him wifely honor as head of the home. The Shunammite appealed to her husband. Nor did she indicate here solo action; she used the "we" approach, enlisting her husband's interest and involvement via a simple, direct request—a request that's spoken just once. Unlike the Shunammite, too many of us wives grab the reins of household leadership, try to steer a husband by hinting or nagging, or stew unhappily in frustration over his nonvision or nonaction.

Second, consider the essence of what the woman of Shunem proposed—a consistent future provision of hospitality. How does that translate? Primarily, it was recognition of need—compassionate concern. Too, it was volunteering for additional responsibility—both in terms of household adjustment and still more work. As mentioned before, the word *work* for her had far tougher meaning than it does for us. Imagine it for a moment. She had to create every dish they were to consume from raw foodstuffs, some of which she no doubt grew in her own garden. Her bread making demanded that she grind her own wheat. Water had to be transported from a well—most likely one located in the village, some distance from her house. She had to hand-process flax and wool and then weave the fabric for her hand-sewn clothing. Housekeeping was done in a structure made of rough stones with a hard-packed dirt floor. Hers was likely the task of milking goats or cows and then making cheese from what was not used otherwise. In short, she lived out the reality of the exhausting list of doings that appears in Proverbs 31—yet she offered to become innkeeper for God's man!

The Shunammite's plan for Elisha essentially moved her into an active ministry. No, she didn't play the piano. She was certainly not married to a preacher! She didn't teach a Sunday school class. She didn't sing solos. She wasn't sallying forth to speak in meetings. Nevertheless, she became active in ministry: the blessed, much-needed ministry of hospitality.

Although she lived long years ago, the Shunammite can remind us of a current reality: people all around us have needs to which we should respond with compassion and practical undertaking. Shunammite-like outreach can soften the hearts of unbelievers and strengthen the hearts of believers.

Is there any Christian woman reading this book who cannot have such a ministry? Is hospitality limited to the preacher's wife or to domestic science majors or to married women or to natural-born cooks or to any age group? The answer to all those questions, of course, is *no*. This wonderful, rare, and blessed ministry of hospitality requires only two things—an open heart and an open home. "But" you may protest, "if I'm to have a hospitality ministry I need . . ." Oh? Look again at verse 10. See how basic she was in thinking of what was needed: "a little chamber"—not a suite, simply a small room that would afford privacy and rest, a bed, a table, a stool, a candlestick. A place to sleep. A table at which to eat or study. A stool on which to sit. A source of light when darkness fell.

Ah, but what do you or I think we need for hostessing? A formal dining room? Fine china? Sterling flatware? Lace-trimmed table linens? Oooops. No wonder so many, many women say to me, "I wish I could have some place of ministry," while all the time they're occupying that very opportunity-filled place. The problem is not lack of opportunity but lack of sightedness. This dear Shunammite destroyed every excuse we may raise against ministry living, didn't she? Well, her story has only begun.

> And it fell on a day that he came thither, and he turned into the chamber, and lay there. And he said to Gehazi his servant, Call this Shunammite. And when he had called her, she stood before him. And he said unto him, Say now unto her, Behold, thou hast been careful for us with all this care; what is to be done for thee? wouldest thou be spoken for to the king, or to the captain of the host? And she answered, I dwell among mine

own people. And he said, What then is to be done for her? And Gehazi answered, Verily she hath no child, and her husband is old. (II Kings 4:11–14)

The guest room was built and furnished, and evidently the Shunammite's hospitality ministry went on for some time. In response to the blessing of the bed and board she provided, Elisha wanted to do something to reciprocate. It's important to realize that when the prophet referred to the king and the captain of the host, he wasn't simply pronouncing titles and positions; he actually had recourse to both those powerful men. But notice this woman's disinterest in repayment, reward, advertisement, or advancement for what she had done. Honesty makes me admit that if I were to receive such an offer, I'd probably jump at the opportunity presented—maybe requesting a little financial help from the government or a chance to see the king's court, or . . . Perhaps the idea of military assistance would be more attractive: a special guard placed around the house because of dangers inherent in the heavily traveled road, or. . .

A recent heart-walk with the Shunammite made me aware of another aspect of her response to Elisha's proffered help: she didn't seek special spiritual rescue, despite the fact that it was his stature as a prophet she appreciated and admired. How easily she could have said, "How about asking God to zap my husband with spirituality?" Or "Put his name on your prayer list for salvation, won't you?" Or "Can't you get my good-for-nothing husband in a corner and try to straighten him out spiritually?"

Acknowledging the contrast between my probable response and the Shunammite's actual one presents me with such powerful rebuke that I want to duck or hide! You and I are quick to seek recognition or reward, aren't we? Not so this dear woman. Her response to the prophet says volumes about her heart:

I live among mine own people.

There is a world of meaning in those few words. In them she expressed utter contentment with her life. My mind goes immediately to I Timothy 6:6—"But godliness with contentment is great gain." What a spiritually wealthy woman, this Shunammite! But the rare, rich quality of her heart becomes even more apparent as you think back over what we've learned of her situation: marriage to a spiritually dead, wholly unimaginative man. Her contentment shows itself to be even more amazing as we move on. But it all comes down to this: she chose to be contented. She focused her heart upon the positive circumstance of dwelling among her own people. Examine the Shunammite's portrait closely at this point: apparently the fact that marriage allowed her to remain close to her own people was the only positive in her life—yet she was content. She uttered not one negative word when given the opportunity to point to, complain about, and express need in multiple empty places. Was this woman made of some material other than human bone, muscle, sinew, and blood? No. But she sublimated things of the flesh to things of the spirit—and thereby experienced and demonstrated Jehovah's effective filling.

Is there any one of us who doesn't struggle in the matter of contentment? In fact, that's what this entire book has dealt with, isn't it? We are discontented in multiple areas of life; we point to and whine or complain about our empty places. How the woman of Shunem shames us!

The statement of contentment, though beautiful, left Elisha floundering: how could he express his gratitude if she wouldn't even mention a need? So Gehazi, Elisha's servant, stepped into the matter. He passed along some information:

Verily she hath no child, and her husband is old.

What had Gehazi just identified? Empty places—two very important empty places! The woman was living with an empty place maritally and an empty place maternally.

"Her husband is old" doesn't only indicate that he was unlikely to sire a child. Apparently the effects of the man's agedness upon the marriage relationship had been so obvious that even a servant recognized them. Let your imagination make the phrase come alive as you put yourself in the Shunammite's place. A young woman married to a much older man probably would have multiple challenges:

- He'd be wrinkled.
- He'd be set in his ways.
- He'd likely be crotchety.
- He'd be impatient with youthful "ignorance."
- He'd be sublevel in romantic impulses and behavior (lacking dentures even to nibble her ear?).

And, in fact, following verses reveal that he was light-years from being love's young dream—he was closer to being a nightmare. Talk about a woman living with marital emptiness, she was it!

Gehazi pointed to another lack in the Shunammite's life: "She hath no child." Maternal emptiness was added to marital emptiness. Her normal womanly desires for childbearing had been thwarted. The culture of the times put tremendous stress upon a woman's fertility. Imagine how greatly she must have longed for a child to love in compensation for her poor marital situation.

Two empty places so glaringly evident that a servant noticed, yet she did not mention them. What a contrast to contemporary feminine mindsets. Women today are quick to speak of marital or maternal empty places. Nor can I just point at others; though I don't make them public, my tiny marital empty places loom large at times, and I do plenty of internal grumbling about them. I remember, too, how immense was the empty maternal yearning for another child after our first baby died and how I focused discontentedly upon my inability to conceive again immediately.

> And he said, Call her. And when he had called her, she stood in the door. (II Kings 4:15)

On the surface this seems an unnecessary and innocuous detail. Not so. God doesn't say anything unnecessary or innocuous. The meaning-filled words here are "she stood in the door." Again, I ask you to engage your imaginative powers. Elisha had made the Shunammite's house a regular stopping place, evidently for a considerable length of time, a sort of B & B. Now remember, this woman is strongly perceptive. As the man of God spent hours visiting, eating at her table, engaging in conversation with her and her husband, she could not have missed noting the vast differences between Elisha and her husband. Elisha towered as a giant personally and spiritually; her husband was just as surely a dwarf in those important areas. What might the obvious distinctions have awakened in her emotionally?

Think it through carefully: empty places in her marital relationship and the resulting painful loneliness, an enormous empty place in her heart through her husband's inability to come alongside her spiritually, a bottomless chasm of emptiness where she yearned to give and receive love, awareness of a man there in the house who was outstanding in so many ways.

Read it again: "And when he had called her, she stood in the door." This spiritually great woman recognized that she was vulnerable: she did not consider herself immune from temptations of the flesh. That's yet another indication of her exceptional wisdom. Godly wisdom not only identifies and moves toward truth and right but also identifies personal, ugly realities inherent in our earthly tabernacle—and buttresses against attack at those places.

Wherefore let him that thinketh he standeth take heed lest he
fall. (I Corinthians 10:12)

Satan could have destroyed the Shunammite right there within
the walls of her home had she not shielded herself against him. She
didn't have to go to a bar or a bordello; opportunity for sin lay close
at hand, so she refused to let her feet enter into a place where temp-
tation might overcome her. She did not go into the prophet's room;
she stopped and stood in the door.

As we have already seen, an empty place can be a place of vulnerability. For the Shunammite, her multiple empty places could
have combined to cry out with fleshly yearning toward Elisha. Too-
close contact with him, or a place of privacy like his bedroom, could
have lured her into emotional adultery, or even physical adultery.
Oh, that God's women today—including ministry women—would
guard themselves so wisely. But all too often both common sense
and spiritual wisdom are cast aside by focusing upon and seeking to
fill empty places, and there begins moral destruction.

As the woman of Shunem wisely stood at the opening of the
prophet's room, Elisha gave her a thank-you gift far beyond anything either king or captain could have bestowed. He promised that
the following year she'd bear a son. She was so overwhelmed by the
prophet's words that she blurted, "Nay my lord, thou man of God,
do not lie unto thy handmaid." The enormity of her surprise can be
clearly heard in those words: she spoke of lies in connection with
the man she hosted as bearer of the truth! Entering that scene in
imagination, I can see the prophet smile as he imparted the wonderful promise from Jehovah.

And the woman conceived, and bare a son at that season that
Elisha had said unto her, according to the time of life. (II Kings
4:17)

We who have borne a child can comprehend something of the Shunammite's joy at the event. But surely her delight knew a breadth and depth beyond what is normally experienced because of the emotional dearth in her marriage. That baby boy opened a whole new world to her. Because of him a song could replace a sigh, empty arms could know warm, delightful filling, ears empty of loving, kind words would fill with gurgles, giggles, and blossoming speech and the blessed pronunciation of "Mama." Rather than a house empty of genuine companionship, she would have reveled in its filling with a little boy's crawling and toddling, running and jumping, hugging and kissing.

But suddenly that gloriously full world was shaken again to emptiness.

> And when the child was grown, it fell on a day, that he went out to his father to the reapers. And he said unto his father, My head, my head. And he said to a lad, Carry him to his mother. And when he had taken him, and brought him to his mother, he sat on her knees till noon, and then died. (II Kings 4:18–20)

The Shunammite had grown used to her son's rich filling of her home and her life. She joyfully beheld his healthy growth. But how shockingly quick came the change. In the brief words given above, Scripture sketches a picture of awful failure in the father and awful loss for the mother. Read it again, and see through the black-and-white type the father's hardheartedness. When the boy cried out in an agony of head pain, his father brushed the complaint aside as he would a bothersome insect. Only the reaping business of the moment mattered; his suffering child he foisted off on a young servant. That uncaring, dismissive action must have stabbed the mother to her heart: having her sick child brought in to her by a lackey was proof positive that her husband lacked all natural affection. The deficiency shown toward their son would have been harder to endure than the husbandly shortfall she had known herself throughout their marriage.

We're told that the boy sat in his mother's lap until noon. The Shunammite's mind and heart must have made multiple trips along torturous emotional paths during that time. Then the beloved boy grew still and cold in her arms—he was dead.

This outstandingly good, godly woman was not exempt from trouble and suffering. No one escapes life's storms. We need to remind ourselves of this fact often, lest we wallow in a bog of self-pity, resentment, and feelings unfairness when trouble sweeps into our own lives.

The heartache experienced by the Shunammite had to have been terrific. Her son had been her prime fulfillment and joy. How slow must have been her steps, how bowed together her physical frame as she carried the boy's body up the stairs and laid him on Elisha's bed.

In the disposal of her son's body and in her actions thereafter, we see the woman again demonstrating both spiritual wisdom and faith: she turned to God for help. There was no hesitation, no period of overpowering bitterness and immobility; no flight to someone in "her own people," important as they evidently were to her. Are you and I so instant and faithful in that God-ward choice when we experience trouble?

The Shunammite again appealed to her husband in order to reach the prophet, and again he fell short in measure as a man.

> And she called unto her husband, and said, Send me, I pray thee, one of the young men, and one of the asses, that I may run to the man of God, and come again. (II Kings 4:22)

Here again we see the propriety and respect with which she spoke to her husband. And notice that she didn't mention the boy's death—their relationship lacked even that modicum of unity. Too, his parental treatment of the boy while he was alive, typified by the coldness of "Carry him to his mother," assured her that whatever reaction he might have would be unhelpful. She was right! Listen to the man's response.

> And he said, Wherefore wilt thou go to him to day? it is neither
> new moon, nor sabbath. And she said, It shall be well. (4:23)

Crotchety and impatient, wholly involved with business and devoid of human warmth, he questioned her spiritually motivated desire, as one who lived a stranger to such motivations. How calmly she responded to his challenge and how admirably she controlled her emotions! In a similar situation I would likely have screamed and kicked the miserable fellow in the shin! Much of the secret behind her restrained, directed emotions peeks out from her ending sentence: "It shall be well." That's quiet, strong faith at work.

> Then she saddled an ass, and said to her servant, Drive, and go
> forward; slack not thy riding for me, except I bid thee. (4:24)

Do you see the subject and verb in the sentence? She had to saddle the donkey herself—her husband wouldn't even do that small, helpful thing for her. Only after she saddled the animal and was ready to start her journey did she feel free to reveal something of the urgency involved. The poor Shunammite could better trust a servant with a glimpse into her heart and the seriousness of the situation than she could her husband!

Elisha saw the woman approaching and sent Gehazi to meet her and ask why she was coming. In response to Gehazi's questioning, the Shunammite merely said, "It is well." Her speaking that phrase at such a moment reveals a great deal about her. As in the instance described earlier, her contentment comes through, but at this later point there's more to be seen in what she said. The contentment that so beautifully marked her life was not an insipid, do-nothing mask for spiritual inertia. As in the very beginning of the passage, here too she actively demonstrated spiritual energy and intent. She was bent upon reaching the prophet—the one whose spiritual reality had been proven. Here again is evidence of her spiritual perception: she did not recognize in Gehazi godly character like that of Elisha. That perception is accurate; a later chapter in II Kings describes Gehazi's selfish deception and the punishment he received: leprosy. How wise she was to refuse to be diverted when she met Elisha's servant. She would not entrust her heart burden to any but the man of God himself. The crisis didn't create her character and faith—it confirmed the reality of both.

> And when she came to the man of God to the hill, she caught him by the feet: but Gehazi came near to thrust her away. And the man of God said, Let her alone; for her soul is vexed within her: and the Lord hath hid it from me, and hath not told me. Then she said, Did I desire a son of my lord? did I not say, Do not deceive me? (4:27–28)

The Shunammite's action, words, and spirit here as she sought the help of Jehovah remind me of the psalmist's: both God-ward-yearning characters were intense in focus and in expression. There's no prettified, "spiritual" talk here. Too, the immensity of emotion driving the woman of Shunem to her knees at Elisha's feet reminds me of Hannah's earlier extremity before Eli the priest.

Elisha responded immediately to the Shunammite's appeal, instructing Gehazi to take the prophet's staff and hurry to her house. He was told to lay the staff upon the child. But again, operating with spiritual discernment, the Shunammite refused the help of any but the prophet himself.

> And the mother of the child said, As the Lord liveth, and as thy soul liveth, I will not leave thee. And he arose, and followed her. (4:30)

The Shunammite's petition and her conduct in this time of immense need are challenging. There's no wild wailing, no mindless emotional explosion, despite the obvious intensity of her heart's hurt. Rather, I see spiritual direction and focus: the statement of her need is clear but brief, her presentation humble. So you and I in our crises should maintain a firm grasp upon our faith. No matter how devastating the situation, God and God alone can make it right. We're to seek Him through His Word and, secondarily, through His proven servants in our times of dire emptiness.

The Shunammite's determined reliance upon the prophet was fully justified: Gehazi went ahead and followed his master's instruction about laying the staff upon the stricken child. But to no avail: the boy remained a prisoner of death. Then the man of God reached the house, and he served as the conduit for Jehovah's miracle-working power:

> He went in therefore, and shut the door upon them twain, and prayed unto the Lord. And he went up, and lay upon the child, and put his mouth upon his mouth, and his eyes upon his eyes, and his hands upon his hands: and he stretched himself upon the child; and the flesh of the child waxed warm. Then he returned, and walked in the house to and fro, and went up, and stretched himself upon him: and the child sneezed seven times, and the child opened his eyes. And he called Gehazi, and said, Call this Shunammite. So he called her. And when she was come in unto him, he said, Take up thy son. (4:33–36)

Scripture does not tell us what the woman did while Elisha was seeking God's restoration of the boy to life, but the indication is that the prophet's actions were done apart from both Gehazi and the mother. Because of everything seen in the Shunammite to this point, I believe she waited quietly in faith—living out the sweet statement made earlier: "It shall be well." She certainly hadn't prostrated herself in an emotional huddle by the door nor shadowed the prophet in his pacing downstairs—Gehazi had to summon her when the miracle was complete.

> Then she went in, and fell at his feet, and bowed herself to the ground, and took up her son, and went out. (4:37)

She had knelt before in supplication; now she went to her knees in gratitude. Consistent, isn't she? In both petitioning and praising she demonstrated humility. You and I may find it easy to kneel when we come to God with a petition—bent knees indicate the earnestness of our desire. But what of our thanksgiving for answered prayer? As I search my own heart and life, I recognize that there is often a different posture in rendering praise: upright and active, as if there's merely delight in knowing that God heard and answered in a way that pleases me. But shouldn't there, instead, be a sense of overwhelming humility as I recognize my unworthiness and God's greatness? Yet another searching question engendered in my heart by God's great woman!

Each time I read the Shunammite's story, too, my mind travels along a sidetrack at this point. What if God had not seen fit to restore life to her beloved son? Because of her wonderful character revealed throughout the passage, and in keeping with the phrase expressing such a key element of her being, "It is well," I'm convinced the Shunammite would have responded in her disappointment as did King David in the time of his child's death.

> And he said, While the child was yet alive, I fasted and wept: for I said, Who can tell whether God will be gracious to me, that the child may live? But now he is dead, wherefore should I fast? can I bring him back again? I shall go to him, but he shall not return to me. (II Samuel 12:22–23)

Both David and the woman of Shunem knew by faith that God in His love, wisdom, and power would do what was best and that He would provide both endurance for and enrichment in whatever earthly empty place they could experience.

So ends the first portion of the Shunammite's story. But God gives us opportunity to look in on her later, as well. The sequel is found in II Kings 8:1–6.

> Then spake Elisha unto the woman, whose son he had restored to life, saying, Arise, and go thou and thine household, and sojourn wheresoever thou canst sojourn: for the Lord hath called for a famine, and it shall also come upon the land seven years. (8:1)

We're not told how much time passed, but in the interim the Shunammite's husband evidently died, leaving her a widow with the responsibility of her son and her household. The woman's hospitality ministry to the prophet through the years was again rewarded as the prophet warned her to flee the coming trouble.

> And the woman arose, and did after the saying of the man of God: and she went with her household, and sojourned in the land of the Philistines seven years. (8:2)

Again, what faith we see in this woman! As she looked out her window at the surrounding fields, there was no visible indication the crops would fail. And the flight Elisha urged would mean leaving the security of her home and her own people, whose nearness had been such a strengthening factor in her life. Too, transporting herself and her household would have been a daunting task. But she responded in obedience—immediately—to God's instruction through the prophet. No arguing. No delay. She did whatever had to be done, and she did so without a single word or indication of reluctance, argument, or complaint.

At the end of the seven years' famine the woman returned to her homeland. However, it was then necessary to petition the king for the return of her property. Just the thought of appearing before the king must have been a fearsome thing for this simple woman; the king's court would have been unlike anything she'd ever known in her entire life. Again, she faced the difficulties. As she entered the king's presence, Gehazi just "happened" to be there; the moment just "happened" to be one in which the king was listening to accounts of Elisha's doings.

> And it came to pass, as he was telling the king how he had restored a dead body to life, that, behold, the woman whose son he had restored to life, cried to the king for her house and for her land. And Gehazi said, My lord, O king, this is the woman, and this is her son, whom Elisha restored to life. And when the king asked the woman, she told him. So the king appointed unto her a certain officer, saying, Restore all that was hers, and all the fruits of the field since the day that she left the land, even until now. (8:5–6)

Does God undertake for and reward His faithful ones? How beautifully the positive answer can be seen in the Shunammite's life. She knew multiple rewards in the earthly sense, but her reward is far greater than her son's restoration to life, her escape from famine, and the return of her lands and crops. An incalculably greater reward has been bestowed upon her because God saw fit to put her in the pages of His Word: a woman so ordinary in her life station that each of us can identify with her but a woman so extraordinary in her faith walk that each of us must be challenged by her. Here she stands—not just through the thousands of years since she lived but on through however many years our globe continues to exist—and, indeed, on into God's glorious eternity.

🌿 THINKING IT OVER 🌿

As you and I have examined the Scripture portrait of the Shunammite, how do we measure up? Clearly, she was a woman who experienced empty places—undeniable lacks in areas of life that are particularly important to a woman. But she was never guilty of useless concentration on or complaint about the emptiness. Instead, she consistently allowed earth's vacancies to be opportunities for heaven's verities.

CHAPTER FOURTEEN

OUR NEEDY HEARTS

LET US HEAR THE CONCLUSION OF THE WHOLE MATTER:
FEAR GOD, AND KEEP HIS COMMANDMENTS: FOR THIS IS THE
WHOLE DUTY OF MAN. FOR GOD SHALL BRING EVERY WORK
INTO JUDGMENT, WITH EVERY SECRET THING, WHETHER IT BE
GOOD OR WHETHER IT BE EVIL.

ECCLESIASTES 12:13–14

Whenever and wherever you and I experience the onset of an emptiness breeze, we need to become spiritual spelunkers and explore the cave from which the unsettling air emanates. If we go into the cave using only mental and emotional sight, we'll see depth and darkness; we'll be convinced that our need is genuine and crucial. We'll be tempted to curl up into ourselves within the cave, engulfed by its echoing expanse. If, however, before we look into the cave we turn to Him Who is light and petition His accompanying, the cave will look far different. Enlightenment will reveal its true character and extent. Our perceived need may instead be lust. We use the word *need* constantly and loosely. In reality, however, as human beings we have few genuine needs for survival:

- Water
- Food
- Shelter
- Clothing
- Companionship

Anything beyond those is a gift—a gift from God. Perhaps if each of us would look at the list of basics each day, we'd be more inclined to gratitude and less to grasping and griping. My off-kilter perception of needs made me tack in front of my computer a little 3 x 5 card with some potent words by George Herbert:

Thou hast given so much to me,
Give one thing more—a grateful heart:
Not thankful when it pleaseth me,
As if Thy blessings had spare days,
But such a heart whose pulse may be
Thy praise.

But think how easily, instead, we expand our needs list:

- Water—piped-in, purified, bottled, iced . . .
- Food—abundant, varied, gourmet, served . . .
- Shelter—roomy, comfortable, professionally decorated, admired . . .
- Clothing—new, fashionable, tailored, designer-labeled . . .
- Companionship—intimate, interesting, pleasant, uncomplicated . . .

Amazing, isn't it? We persistently want more. God in His grace has literally loaded us with benefits (Psalm 68:19), but we hardly see them because our eyes are set upon things beyond, better, or above. Aren't we, then, in God's terms, lusting?

If it weren't for our lustful hearts, we'd experience far fewer empty places. If we would awaken to and be grateful for our wholly undeserved blessings, how different our spirit, homes, churches, and even nation would be. But we Christians long ago enrolled in America's consumer culture. Its credo is "I want, I deserve, and I'll go after." In essence, we've become idolators. We bow daily at the altar of materialism and worship the many-armed goddess of self. That's a sad, destructive choice. No fullness can be found at the altar, and no satisfaction in the hands of self.

> All the labour of man is for his mouth, and yet the appetite is not filled. (Ecclesiastes 6:7)

THE END OF OUR EMPTY PLACES

The woman of Shunem certainly can serve as model and rebuke for each of us modern-day Christian women. But as we keep her image before us, how can we translate her example of spiritual success into our complex twenty-first-century life?

We need not approach the challenge with reservation because we see the Shunammite as colossal; rather, we can recognize her as fully human—yet exemplifying wonderful fullness. Consider, too, that she lived in the Old Testament era, which meant that her faith had to reach forward into the future. The coming of Jesus Christ, the Messiah, lay hundreds of years away from her. Christ had not yet completed the transaction of salvation through His death and resurrection. The Holy Spirit had not yet been made the blessed In-dweller of each believer. Whatever portion of Scripture might have been available to her was just that—a portion. God's written Word was far smaller than that available to you and me today. Her faith would have been bolstered primarily by recognizing the meaning of redemption that was signified in the sacrifice of animals as prescribed by the law. Much knowledge of Jehovah's specific dealings depended upon the prophets He commissioned—like Elijah and Elisha, those preaching during her era. Despite all those difficulties, that dear woman of Shunem set her heart upon the God of Israel; she conformed her self and conducted her life according to His law and for His pleasure.

The spiritual resources at hand for you and me today are immeasurably richer. The written Word is complete and easily available to each of us. That blessed book contains a complete supply for our every need. We have faithful, true-to-the-Word evangelists, pastors, and teachers throughout the land. Each of us personally receives the Holy Spirit to dwell within us the moment we accept Christ as Savior. Prophecy has been fulfilled and the Messiah has come; Jesus Christ has lived and died, the perfect Lamb of God through Whose shed blood we're cleansed and brought into the family of God.

Despite all those spiritual riches so readily at hand, few Christian women live richly; we more typically choose to ignore the abundance offered. Instead, we focus upon and are reduced by life's supposed empty places.

What, then, is the crucial factor for any of us wishing to know fullness of life? It's certainly not found in self, except in that we each must choose to make the factor operational. To put it simply, the spiritual success—the fullness—of your life and mine depends upon our heart's address.

Our Lord Jesus Christ long ago identified the place of residence He desires for you and me.

Abide in me. (John 15:4)

That invitation is familiar as a statement, but it's rare as a consistent experience. How recently have you let the tiny, potent phrase permeate your mind and put its roots deep into your heart? Let's allow it to do so together.

THE INVITATION

How gracious are the Savior's words! They remind us of His invitation to salvation.

> Come unto me, all ye that labour and are heavy laden, and I will give you rest. (Matthew 11:28)

Without that original coming, of course, we cannot go on to respond to this further invitation to dwell in Him. We are accepted in the beloved at the instant of salvation, but we abide in Him by a heart choice moment by moment.

Why should we make the choice to abide in Christ? Because apart from His protection, provision, and sustaining, enemies within and without will defeat us.

> My flesh and my heart faileth: but God is the strength of my heart, and my portion for ever. (Psalm 73:26)

The psalmist also pictures for us the completeness of our refuge.

> My soul, wait thou only upon God; for my expectation is from him. He only is my rock and my salvation: he is my defence; I shall not be moved. In God is my salvation and my glory: the rock of my strength, and my refuge, is in God. (Psalm 62:5–7)

That mighty Refuge, however, doesn't demand our taking up residence in Him. In keeping with His love, which allows our free choice for acquaintanceship with Him by salvation, so too with abiding in Him: we take on that address by asking,

> Be thou my strong habitation, whereunto I may continually resort: thou hast given commandment to save me; for thou art my rock and my fortress (Psalm 71:3).

Although each of us ought to have the perception of our need to abide in Christ, familiarity, longevity, and forgetfulness can conspire to deaden us to that essential. Three brief passages from Psalm 74 can effectively reawaken our awareness.

The dark places of the earth are full of the habitations of cruelty. (74:20*b*)

Every newspaper and each television news broadcast highlight the accuracy of that description of the world at large, doesn't it. More and more we're told of kidnap, rape, murder, terrorism, and moral mayhem around the globe. Unthinkable cruelties are epidemic: children murdering parents and grandparents, parents torturing their children, employees blasting away at fellow workers and employers, students decimating their schoolrooms with gunfire, drivers riddling the cars of other drivers who innocently offend them in traffic.

Too, there is inescapable evidence of mounting hatred against true Christianity.

The tumult of those that rise up against thee increaseth continually. (Psalm 74:23*b*)

While general talk of God may receive little more than a shrug, the name of Jesus Christ brings instant, bitter protest. The spiritual atmosphere of America has changed drastically since the days of its founding upon biblical principles. There is a push throughout our society to reject Christianity while accommodating Eastern belief, mysticism, aberrant philosophy, and crackpot "freethink." There is a rush toward inclusivism and tolerance—as long as they stand apart from any Bible connection. Voices raised against truth grow louder and angrier day by day.

Even more distressing than the unsaved world's antagonism is the spiritual disintegration within Christianity itself.

Thine enemies roar in the midst of thy congregations; they set
up their ensigns for signs. (Psalm 74:4)

There is hardly a solid, Bible-preaching church anywhere that is
not experiencing this sad reality. Satan has infiltrated our ranks; his
emissaries display the accoutrements of light, but they act in behalf
of darkness. The roar of their voice grows louder each day, and the
vehemence of their spirit confuses and draws away those who are
weak in their spiritual rooting. Their ensigns are "private interpre-
tation" of Scripture—banners of their own making—

- Theological system preferences
- Peripheral personal "standards" demands
- Illogical, unhistorical textual claims
- Dietary programs claiming spiritual brownie points
- Extreme exaltation of home and family
- Antigovernment beliefs and practices
- Any number of other petty, divisive emphases

The fallout from the waving of such ensigns is drastic: personal
polarizations that damage church unity, undercurrents of disagreement and criticism, gossip outside the church that harms the public's trust and the church's testimony, dissatisfied church members
playing church hopscotch, wounded church members changing to
liberal denominations, gossip-battered church leaders opting out of
further service, embittered young people throwing over all respect
for and connection with the church. No wonder God states repeatedly in His Word that He hates divisiveness.

Each of us needs to seek the Lord's wisdom in order to discern
between separation and divisiveness. From His first dealings with
Israel through the close of Revelation God indeed calls His people
to be separated—separated unto Him. Divisiveness draws people
apart—period—and is marked by bitter self-righteousness.

The escalation of troubles facing us everywhere should not move us to check out and hide but rather to check up and abide. We should never take our spiritual condition for granted; it can cool and weaken far too easily. We need to obey the Scripture's repeated reminder "Take heed to thyself." So, then, in view of the challenges facing us, where do we abide—what's our spiritual address? Different (honest) answers may apply:

- Rationality Ranch
- Emotion Estates
- Complacency Corner
- Fearful Forest Avenue
- Bluff-Em Boulevard
- Inconsistency Condos
- Modernity Mews
- Anxiety Apartments
- Denominational Label Lane
- Self Slums

Whether we admit an inferior address, we can be sure the location is accurately recorded in God's address book! Where any heart address other than "In Him" applies, our heavenly Father must sigh His disappointment over the empty places we create for ourselves by choosing the wrong dwelling place.

Scripture makes it clear that when we rightly abide in Jesus Christ, we have access to an incalculable, absolutely limitless supply for our every need. Each time we dig into precious Bible phrases such as "He is . . . ," ". . . in whom . . . ," "In Him . . ." we're reminded of spiritual riches beyond any oil, gas, or gold discoveries ever found on earth. As just a tiny indication of those riches, think back over the following.

But of him are ye in Christ Jesus, who of God is made unto us
wisdom, and righteousness, and sanctification, and redemption.
(I Corinthians 1:30)

For it pleased the Father that in him should all fullness dwell.
(Colossians 1:19)

For he is our peace. (Ephesians 2:14)

In whom are hid all the treasures of wisdom and knowledge.
(Colossians 2:3)

For in him dwelleth all the fullness of the Godhead bodily.
(Colossians 2:9)

With those few references alone we can be jolted to realize how
foolish we are ever to dwell apart from Him!

But let's go on and drill our way into yet another lode of truth—
where, with every tiny thrusting of our mind, we can see the
twenty-four-karat supply God maintains for you and me at His
address.

And God is able to make all grace abound toward you; that ye,
always having all sufficiency in all things, may abound to every
good work. (II Corinthians 9:8)

As we begin to search out the meaning of the words and phrases,
we can divide them into three categories: promising, providing, and
producing.

Promising "all grace"

And what is grace? It's God's undertaking for us, His enabling of
us, His limitless power replacing our helplessness. Nor is that ever-
rich supply parceled out in dribs and drabs: He tells us that He
extends to us "all grace." Yet how consistently I miss that supply
because He delivers to only one address.

PROMISING "ABOUNDING GRACE"

It's as if God comes back with a highlighter, knowing that our earth-dull brains excel in missing what He communicates: His ever-available grace is so wonderfully rich that it's the shaken-down, full-to-running-over kind—not just sufficient for our needs but overflowingly so.

PROVIDING "ALWAYS"

Here God addresses time as it relates to His supply. The hands on our clocks can never point to any second, minute, or hour in which we do not have access to His enabling. Yet I manage to limit the supply, relegating it to particularly intense or big moments, attempting at other times to manage on my own pitiful supply via self.

PROVIDING "ALL SUFFICIENCY"

Sufficiency has always been a difficult term for me, an unreachable state of being and doing. Looking back even into childhood, I recognize enormous personal ineptitude and uncertainty. Growth in the truth has been painfully slow, belatedly bringing me to the marvelous realization that my sufficiency isn't meant to be mine; rather it's to be His in-pouring. And look at that little descriptive word *all*. Again I can sense God's wish to highlight for me—to focus my myopic spiritual gaze upon the glorious boundlessness of His offered supply.

PROVIDING "ALL THINGS"

Here the Lord points into our life, declaring that any endeavor we undertake in His will we can successfully accomplish by His sustaining.

As I sit at the computer trying to make progress on this "thing" of my manuscript and sense His enabling grace, my mind races away across the miles to a precious friend to whom I spoke just moments ago on the telephone. Her "thing" is far different from mine: not a quiet, solo writing endeavor but the heart-tearing experience of walking beside her beloved husband as he moves through the painful valley of death's shadows. Yet her narrative was filled with laughter and her vocal timbre communicated assurance. Oh, blessed reminder of the Lord's sufficiency for our every "thing." And what a potent reminder of what we miss when we choose the wrong address!

Producing "abounding good work"

When we rightly abide in Christ, the work of our hands—whatever it may be—will be a good work. Our unity with Him, our control and direction by the Holy Spirit, will make a ministry of our life. As we conform to His will, He will be able to pronounce our every work "good"—just as He did of His creative works long ago. Genuine good works lack the dragging, darkening ingredients of self-motivation, self-energizing, and self-glorification; instead, all is of and for Him.

The apostle Paul was one who wonderfully maintained his spiritual address; his abiding in Christ is evident in everything Scripture tells of him. Although admittedly human, Paul took up spiritual residence in Christ the moment he met Him on the Damascus road, and he never abandoned—or even vacationed from—that address. It was thus he was able to say in Ephesians 3:7,

> Whereof I was made a minister, according to the gift of the grace
> of God given unto me by the effectual working of his power.

Of all God's representatives who appear in the New Testament, none was more mighty in life and in works than Paul. But at every opportunity he pointed away from himself. He wanted all attention and honor to go to the God of grace and the grace of God.

Proper abiding in Christ has a unique spirit. John 17 lets us listen in on Jesus' agonized prayer in Gethsemane's darkness. Kneeling alone before He had to stumble, cross-laden, to Golgotha, our Savior prayed earnestly for His disciples. Moreover, He makes it clear that the prayer was not only for those in the original group but for you and me as well.

> Neither pray I for these alone, but for them also which shall believe on me through their word. (John 17:20)

And this was His prayer.

> That they all may be one; as thou, Father, art in me, and I in thee, that they also may be one in us: that the world may believe that thou hast sent me. (John 17:21)

Each time I come to this beautiful prayer I choke with emotion as it so clearly reveals the Savior's heart of love. He longed for us who believe in Him to demonstrate loving unity with one another. Think for a moment about what Jesus was saying as He prayed for us to be united in Him. Listen again to the words of His prayer.

When we Christians demonstrate love one for another, our love-worked unity is reflective: it shows to the world something of the Godhead's unity—"As thou, Father, art in me, and I in thee . . ." Considering the paucity of Christian unity now evident in our Bible-believing circles, it's no wonder the world increasingly mocks the idea of a triune God! In fact, it's really no wonder the world increasingly mocks the existence of any God at all. Our representation of Him is shameful in its every aspect.

Too, Christian unity, according to Jesus' prayer, is meant to be recognized: it shows to the world that Jesus Christ is indeed the Messiah, the One sent from God—"That the world may believe that thou hast sent me." How might such a validation come through our unity? Because such bonding is possible only through love—God's love active in and flowing from us. Human beings do not naturally opt for or experience unity. Instead, self-advancement and others-stomping are programmed into our cells. If we Christians lived in genuine, loving unity, the world would be shocked into recognizing those relationships as being otherworldly. Think what a powerful magnet that would create for the Lord. In fact, we know the power of that magnet—it's recorded in Scripture and in history, as vibrant Christian love has drawn unnumbered souls to Jesus Christ. Tragically today, though, our treatment of one another is like that among the unsaved—and sometimes worse.

So, Christian, draw near again—alone—to Jesus praying there in the garden. Hear the moaning prayer He lifts to His Father. Listen closely to His heart revealed. Then measure your own heart against His mighty one. Aren't you challenged about your spiritual address, your love for others, and your spirit toward your family of believers? I certainly am! I'm forced to admit, with shame, that rather than having a permanent address, mine more resembles motor-home living.

But there is more to genuine abiding in Christ than love for the brethren. Love can be—and is—counterfeited. Sweet words, syrupy tones, and exalted facial expressions are not difficult to produce. But God asks far more of us: He asks reality and full-self, whole-life involvement.

Although many passages of Scripture can be quoted, Psalm 15 gives us just a glimpse of what our spiritual address demands. The passage opens with a direct question about address-identifying characteristics:

> Lord, who shall abide in thy tabernacle? and who shall dwell in thy holy hill?

The answer comes immediately and clearly, and it covers a broad spectrum of spiritual responsibilities: "He that walketh uprightly." Of course there is no uprightness possible apart from Christ's bestowment of His own righteousness upon us as we come to Him for salvation. It all starts there, and everything thereafter indicates the presence or absence of that fountainhead. Walking uprightly after we've been to the cross is walking in daily obedience to God's Word—all of it.

"And worketh righteousness." Walking uprightly is the personal posture we're to maintain; working righteousness is the product of our hands validating the posture of our soul.

"And speaketh the truth in his heart." The one who abides in Christ is marked by through-and-through integrity. There is no hypocrisy, no disagreement between the claimed name and reality.

"He that backbiteth not with his tongue." Yipes. How did such a little thing as gossip get into this exalted passage? By its true, monstrous nature, that's how. Although you and I joke about and excuse our tale-telling tongues, God views them as deadly entities (James 3:6). Loose tongues are not to be characteristic of one who abides in Christ.

"Nor doeth evil to his neighbor." Of course we know from Jesus' story of the Good Samaritan that one's "neighbor" is not just the person who lives next door to us. Rather, it's any and every other human being. We would doubtless consider thievery, assault, and murder to be unneighborly evils—and we're horrified to think of being involved in them. But God's "evil" label is far more widely applied. He calls evil anything other than good done to those around us.

"Nor taketh up a reproach against his neighbour." Maybe ours is not a tongue problem so much as an ear problem—listening to gossip, believing the negatives, forming opinions, altering attitudes, and molding treatment of the "newsworthy" person according to what was heard. We thereby "take up a reproach" against that person.

"In whose eyes a vile person is contemned [despised]." This requirement is particularly appropriate for the day in which we live. Vileness flourishes all around us. Its presence and strength are inescapably evident. But Christians have allowed themselves to become desensitized. Generally speaking, we not only tolerate but also imitate moral, ethical, and relational wretchedness. Only two areas of life need to be considered in order to be reminded of our failure to despise vileness: fashion and entertainment. Designers with perverted minds and lives have stripped feminine beauty from fashion—but Christian young people lust after the latest look, and their parents allow and justify their clothing choices, no matter how sloppy, crude, or immodest. Music and films are dominated by individuals whose lowlife examples might make an orangutan blush. Words and action presented are filthy. Yet their abominable products in sound, color, and motion are regularly plugged into the ears and welcomed into the homes of Christians. How can we who claim to be abiding in Christ delight in vileness instead of despising it?

"But he honoureth them that fear the Lord." Here again we miss the mark of proper abiding. There is scant honor one for another and painfully little honor toward those whom God has placed over us in leadership. Instead, churches are filled with scrapping and sniping, accusation and rebellion.

"He that sweareth to his own hurt, and changeth not." We are to be keepers of our word. That concept is generally foreign to modern Christianity, isn't it? People promise all sorts of things in response to all sorts of requests—but they think nothing of reneging. This lack of trustworthiness can be seen in many venues, but the ones I most often observe personally are in the social and financial realms. A person commits to attend an event, the hosting party plans accordingly expending effort and money, but then the invited guest just fails to show, thinking nothing of the broken promise. Or a person signs a loan agreement with a Christian school in order for himself or a child to attend. After the education has been completed, however, loan payment requests are ignored, shrugged off as being of no consequence. If the school has to engage a collection agency, the debtor screams in protest, accusing the school of being un-Christian!

"He that putteth not out his money to usury." The "Christian" promoter who fattens his pockets by "seeding" a project and then luring people into questionable investments or memberships violates this principle for abiding in the Lord.

"Nor taketh reward against the innocent." Probably none of us has ever done this in the sense of unjustly giving over someone to authorities and collecting a reward. But how about using other means to profit from someone's trouble? In the case of a church shakeup like that mentioned earlier, in which a person in leadership is vilified and opposed through gossip, innuendo, or outright rebellion, would you or I "take reward against the innocent" by using his or her ousting as a step up for ourselves?

"He that doeth these things shall never be moved." Now there's a permanent address! But go back—carefully and prayerfully—over the requirements for such residence; recheck the accuracy of your qualifications for the address, Abiding in Christ.

Blessed, blessed abiding: dwelling in that place—that absolutely unique place—wherein is no emptiness.

> And my people shall be satisfied with my goodness, saith the Lord. (Jeremiah 31:14)

> For I have satiated the weary soul, and I have replenished every sorrowful soul. (Jeremiah 31:25)

> He that dwelleth in the secret place of the most High shall abide under the shadow of the Almighty. (Psalm 91:1)

> Blessed is the man whom thou choosest, and causest to approach unto thee, that he may dwell in thy courts: we shall be satisfied with the goodness of thy house, even of thy holy temple. (Psalm 65:4)

Our choice of that place to abide, and our realization of its inexplicable fullness, are motivated by love. Madame Guyon long ago penned a beautiful expression of such love and abiding in "Adoration."

> I love my God, but with no love of mine,
> For I have none to give;
> I love Thee, Lord, but all the love is Thine,
> For by Thy love I live.
> I am as nothing, and rejoice to be
> Emptied and lost and swallowed up in Thee.
> Thou, Lord, alone art all Thy children need,
> And there is none beside;
> From Thee the streams of blessedness proceed,
> In Thee the blest abide—
> Fountain of life and all-abounding grace,
> Our source, our center, and our dwelling place.

THINKING IT OVER

Empty places are experienced by every one of us here on earth. But they remain empty only if we choose to have it so. Each of our empty places presents a crucial choice: will we let it be a means of crippling or of crowning? Of agonizing or of abiding? Empty places disappear in the Lord Jesus Christ.

> For of him, and through him, and to him, are all things: to whom be glory for ever. (Romans 11:36)

It is He and only He Who *filleth all in all.*

> Now the God of peace, that brought again from the dead our Lord Jesus, that great shepherd of the sheep, through the blood of the everlasting covenant, make you perfect [mature] in every good work to do his will, working in you that which is

wellpleasing in his sight, through Jesus Christ; to whom be glory for ever and ever. Amen. (Hebrews 13:20–21)

Now unto him that is able to keep you from falling, and to present you faultless before the presence of his glory with exceeding joy, to the only wise God our Savior, be glory and majesty, dominion and power, both now and ever. Amen. (Jude 24–25)